SCIENCE
FUSION

fusion [FYOO • zhuhn] a combination of two or more things that releases energy

This **Interactive Student Edition** belongs to

_____

Teacher/Room

_____

HOLT McDOUGAL

 HOUGHTON MIFFLIN HARCOURT

Consulting Authors

Michael A. DiSpezio

Global Educator
North Falmouth, Massachusetts

Michael DiSpezio is a renaissance educator who moved from the research laboratory of a Nobel Prize winner to the K–12 science classroom. He has authored or co-authored numerous textbooks and written more than 25 trade books. For nearly a decade he worked with the JASON Project, under the auspices of the National Geographic Society, where he designed curriculum, wrote lessons, and hosted dozens of studio and location broadcasts. Over the past two decades, he has developed supplementary material for organizations and shows that include PBS *Scientific American Frontiers, Discover* magazine, and the Discovery Channel. He has extended his reach outside the United States and into topics of crucial importance today. To all his projects, he brings his extensive background in science and his expertise in classroom teaching at the elementary, middle, and high school levels.

Marjorie Frank

*Science Writer and
Content-Area Reading Specialist*
Brooklyn, New York

An educator and linguist by training, a writer and poet by nature, Marjorie Frank has authored and designed a generation of instructional materials in all subject areas, including past HMH Science programs. Her other credits include authoring science issues of an award-winning children's magazine; writing game-based digital assessments in math, reading, and language arts; and serving as instructional designer and co-author of pioneering school-to-work software for Classroom Inc., a nonprofit organization dedicated to improving reading and math skills for middle and high school learners. She wrote lyrics and music for *SCIENCE SONGS,* which was an American Library Association nominee for notable recording. In addition, she has served on the adjunct faculty of Hunter, Manhattan, and Brooklyn Colleges, teaching courses in science methods, literacy, and writing.

Acknowledgments for Covers

Front cover: *Polar bear* (bg) ©Mark Rodger-Snelson/Alamy; *false color x-rays on hand* (l) ©Lester Lefkowitz/Getty Images; *primate* (cl) ©Bruno Morandi/The Image Bank/Getty Images; *red cells* (cr) ©Todd Davidson/Getty Images; *fossils* (r) ©Yoshihi Tanaka/amana images/Getty Images

Michael R. Heithaus

Director, School of Environment
and Society
Associate Professor, Department of
Biological Sciences
Florida International University
North Miami, Florida

Mike Heithaus joined
the Florida International
University Biology Department
in 2003. He has served as Director of the Marine
Sciences Program and is now Director of the School
of Environment and Society, which brings together
the natural and social sciences and humanities
to develop solutions to today's environmental
challenges. While earning his doctorate, he began
the research that grew into the Shark Bay Ecosystem
Project in Western Australia, with which he still
works. Back in the United States, he served as a
Research Fellow with National Geographic, using
remote imaging in his research and hosting a 13-
part *Crittercam* television series on the National
Geographic Channel. His current research centers
on predator-prey interactions among vertebrates,
such as tiger sharks, dolphins, dugongs, sea turtles,
and cormorants.

Donna M. Ogle

Professor of Reading and Language
National-Louis University
Chicago, Illinois

Creator of the well-known
KWL strategy, Donna Ogle
has directed many staff
development projects
translating theory and
research into school practice in middle and
secondary schools throughout the United States.
She is a past president of the International Reading
Association and has served as a consultant
on literacy projects worldwide. Her extensive
international experience includes coordinating the
Reading and Writing for Critical Thinking Project in
Eastern Europe, developing an integrated curriculum
for a USAID Afghan Education Project, and speaking
and consulting on projects in several Latin American
countries and in Asia. Her books include *Coming
Together as Readers; Reading Comprehension:
Strategies for Independent Learners; All Children
Read;* and *Literacy for a Democratic Society.*

Program Reviewers

Content Reviewers

Paul D. Asimow, PhD
*Professor of Geology
and Geochemistry*
Division of Geological and
Planetary Sciences
California Institute of Technology
Pasadena, CA

Laura K. Baumgartner, PhD
Postdoctoral Researcher
Molecular, Cellular, and
Developmental Biology
University of Colorado
Boulder, CO

Eileen Cashman, PhD
Professor
Department of Environmental
Resources Engineering
Humboldt State University
Arcata, CA

Hilary Clement Olson, PhD
Research Scientist Associate V
Institute for Geophysics, Jackson
School of Geosciences
The University of Texas at Austin
Austin, TX

Joe W. Crim, PhD
Professor Emeritus
Department of Cellular Biology
The University of Georgia
Athens, GA

Elizabeth A. De Stasio, PhD
*Raymond H. Herzog Professor
of Science*
Professor of Biology
Department of Biology
Lawrence University
Appleton, WI

Dan Franck, PhD
Botany Education Consultant
Chatham, NY

Julia R. Greer, PhD
*Assistant Professor of Materials
Science and Mechanics*
Division of Engineering and
Applied Science
California Institute of Technology
Pasadena, CA

John E. Hoover, PhD
Professor
Department of Biology
Millersville University
Millersville, PA

William H. Ingham, PhD
Professor (Emeritus)
Department of Physics and
Astronomy
James Madison University
Harrisonburg, VA

Charles W. Johnson, PhD
*Chairman, Division of Natural
Sciences, Mathematics, and
Physical Education*
Associate Professor of Physics
South Georgia College
Douglas, GA

© Houghton Mifflin Harcourt Publishing Company

Program Reviewers (continued)

Contents
in Brief

The male frigate bird displays his red throat pouch to attract a mate.

We can study the hair and skin of this woolly mammoth because it was preserved in ice.

Contents

Amber fossils form when small creatures become trapped in tree sap that hardens.

There were all kinds of plants during the Paleozoic era. All except flowering plants that is, which hadn't developed yet.

© Houghton Mifflin Harcourt Publishing Company • Image Credits: (t) ©Howard Grey/Stone/Getty Images; (b) ©Publiphoto/Photo Researchers, Inc.

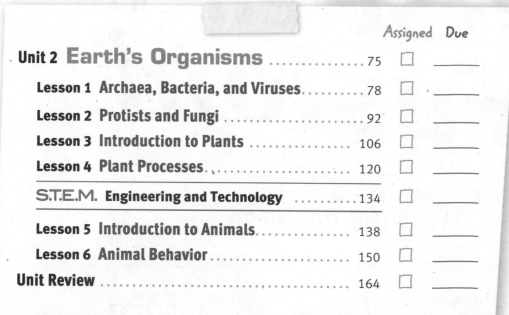

Back off! That's what male Anolis lizards mean when they puff out their colorful throat flaps.

It isn't a vegetable! Pangolins are animals. They use their long, sticky tongues to gather ants and termites.

Assignments:

_____
_____
_____
_____
_____
_____
_____
_____
_____
_____

Power up with Science Fusion!

Your program fuses...

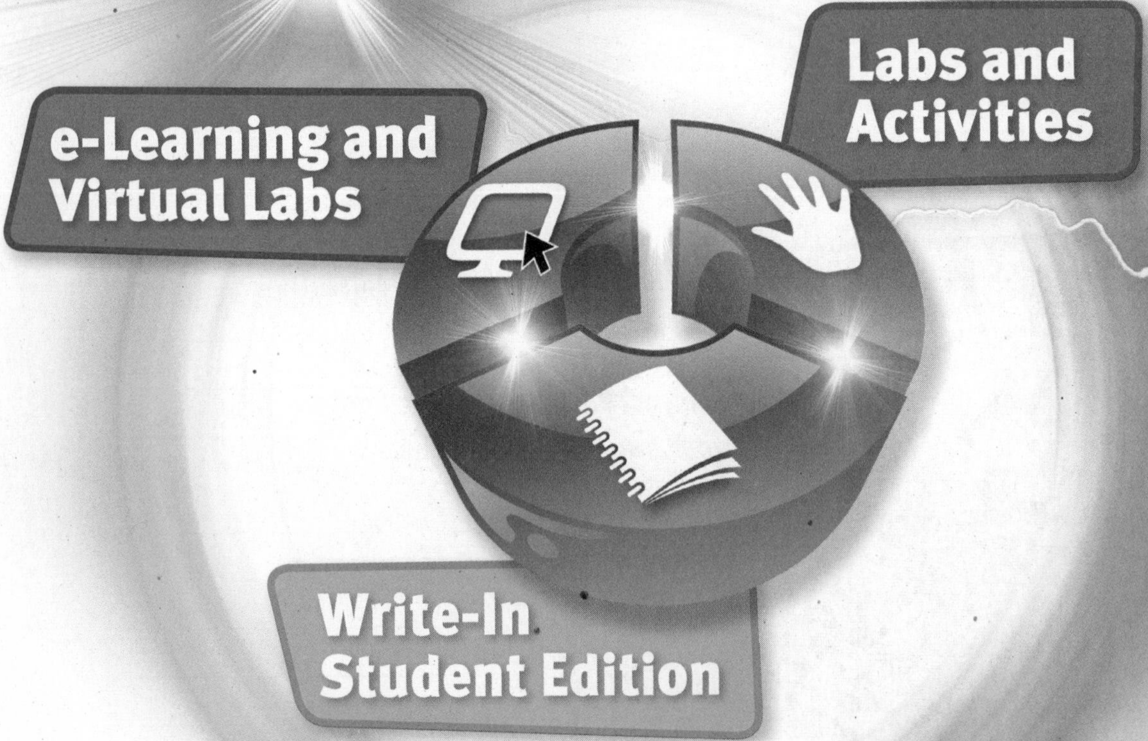

e-Learning and Virtual Labs

Labs and Activities

Write-In Student Edition

...to generate energy for today's science learner — *you*.

Labs and Activities

ScienceFusion includes lots of exciting hands-on inquiry labs and activities, each one designed to bring science skills and concepts to life and get you involved.

By asking questions, testing your ideas, organizing and analyzing data, drawing conclusions, and sharing what you learn...

You are the scientist!

e-Learning and Virtual Labs

Digital lessons and virtual labs provide e-learning options for every lesson of Science Fusion.

On your own or with a group, explore science concepts in a digital world.

360° of Inquiry

Life over Time

Big Idea

The types and characteristics of organisms change over time.

Fossils provide valuable information about life over time. Some species, such as the ginkgo tree, have lived on Earth for millions of years.

What do you think?

Over Earth's history, life forms change as the environment changes. What kinds of organisms lived in your area during prehistoric times?

Modern ginkgo leaf

Unit 1
Life over Time

Prehistoric Life

Scientists have learned a lot about prehistoric times from fossils. We know that life on Earth was very different in the geologic past, and that it changes over time. A changing environment causes changes in the types of organisms that are able to survive.

Jurassic Period
206 m.y.a.–140 m.y.a.

The central United States was covered by a huge ocean during the age of the dinosaurs! Many fossils from that time period are from aquatic organisms.

Mosasaurs found in the Midwest are fossils of extinct marine reptiles.

What clues does this fossil give you about the type of food the animal ate?

Wood fossilizes when minerals replace all the organic material.

Mammals such as this saber-toothed cat once roamed Indiana grasslands.

Great white egrets live in Indiana's wetlands.

Tertiary Period
65 m.y.a.–2 m.y.a.

Land began to emerge from the water. Early mammals and some plants left many kinds of fossils behind, telling us a lot about this period.

Early Holocene
12,000–10,000 years ago

As humans occupied the land, many large animals, including mammoths, mastodons, saber-toothed cats, and giant sloths, disappeared.

Present Day
Humans have a large impact on the organisms living in the Midwest. Some species, such as the piping plover, are threatened with extinction due to human activities. Protecting these species helps to ensure that Midwestern habitats will remain diverse.

Take It Home · Your Neighborhood over Time

Your neighborhood has also changed over time. Do some research to find out when your town was founded. Create a timeline similar to the one above that shows the details of what changes your neighborhood and town might have experienced in the time since it was founded.

Introduction to Living Things

ESSENTIAL QUESTION

What are living things?

By the end of this lesson, you should be able to describe the necessities of life and the characteristics that all living things share.

Living things need energy to survive. This bluebird gets energy by eating insects like this dragonfly.

Engage Your Brain

1 Compare Both of these pictures show living things. How are these living things different?

_____

_____

_____

_____

_____

2 List Many of the things that people need to stay alive are not found in space. List the things that the International Space Station must have to keep astronauts alive.

_____

_____

_____

_____

_____

_____

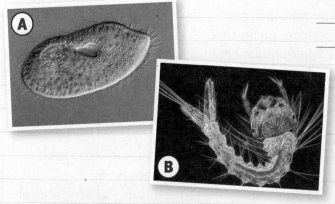

Active Reading

3 Synthesize Many English words have their roots in other languages. Use the Greek words below to make an educated guess about the meaning of the word *homeostasis*.

Greek word	Meaning
hómoios	similar
stásis	standing still

Example sentence

On a hot day, your body sweats to maintain homeostasis.

homeostasis:

_____

_____

Vocabulary Terms
- cell
- stimulus
- homeostasis
- DNA
- sexual reproduction
- asexual reproduction

4 Identify This list contains the vocabulary terms you'll learn in this lesson. As you read, underline the definition of each term.

Share and Share Alike

This is a microscopic view of cells in an onion root. An onion has many cells, so it is a multicellular organism.

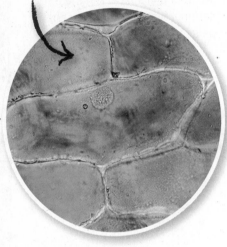

What characteristics do living things share?

An amazing variety of living things exists on Earth. These living things may seem very different, but they are all alike in several ways. What does a dog have in common with a bacterium? What does a fish have in common with a mushroom? There are five characteristics that all living things share.

Living Things Are Made of Cells

All living things are made of one or more cells. A **cell** is a membrane-covered structure that contains all of the materials necessary for life. Cells are the smallest unit of life, which means they are the smallest structures that can perform life functions. Most cells are so small they cannot be seen without a microscope. The membrane that surrounds a cell separates the cell's contents from its environment. Unicellular organisms are made up of only one cell. Multicellular organisms are made up of more than one cell. Some of these organisms have trillions of cells! Cells in a multicellular organism usually perform specialized functions.

Visualize It!

5 Categorize Identify each organism in the picture as unicellular or multicellular.

I'm an amoeba. I am:
☐ unicellular   ☐ multicellular

I'm a cattail. I am:
☐ unicellular   ☐ multicellular

I'm a turtle. I am:
☐ unicellular   ☐ multicellular

Living Things Respond to Their Environment

All living things have the ability to sense change in their environment and to respond to that change. A change that affects the activity of an organism is called a **stimulus** (plural: stimuli). A stimulus can be gravity, light, sound, a chemical, hunger, or anything else that causes an organism to respond in some way. For example, when your pupils are exposed to light—a stimulus—they become smaller—a response.

Even though an organism's outside environment may change, conditions inside its body must stay relatively constant. Many chemical reactions keep an organism alive. These reactions can only happen when conditions are exactly right. An organism must maintain stable internal conditions to survive. The maintenance of a stable internal environment is called **homeostasis**. Your body maintains homeostasis by sweating when it gets hot and shivering when it gets cold. Each of these actions keeps the body at a stable internal temperature.

Visualize It!

6 Analyze Why are these sunflowers all facing in the same direction?

_____

_____

_____

_____

Dogs respond to stimuli in their environment.

7 Infer Fill in the response that a dog might have to each stimulus listed in the table.

Stimulus	Response
Hunger	
Hot Day	
Owner with Leash	
Squirrel in Yard	
Friendly Dog	
Stranger	

Living Things Reproduce

Active Reading 8 **Identify** As you read, underline the ways in which organisms reproduce.

How does the world become filled with plants, animals, and other living things? Organisms make other organisms through the process of reproduction. When organisms reproduce, they pass copies of all or part of their DNA to their offspring. **DNA**, or deoxyribonucleic acid, is the genetic material that controls the structure and function of cells. DNA is found in the cells of all living things. Offspring share characteristics with their parents because they receive DNA from their parents.

Living things reproduce in one of two ways. Two parents produce offspring that share the characteristics of both parents through the process of **sexual reproduction**. Each offspring receives part of its DNA from each parent. Most animals and plants reproduce using sexual reproduction.

A single parent produces offspring that are identical to the parent through the process of **asexual reproduction**. Each offspring receives an exact copy of the parent's DNA. Most unicellular organisms and some plants and animals reproduce using asexual reproduction. Two methods of asexual reproduction are binary fission and budding. A unicellular organism splits into two parts during binary fission. During budding, a new organism grows on the parent organism until it is ready to separate.

A father pig is needed to produce piglets.

Visualize It!

9 **Identify** Use the check boxes to identify which offspring are identical to the parent or parents and which offspring are not identical.

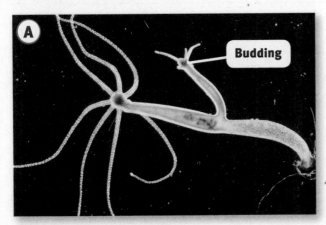

A
Budding

B

A hydra produces offspring using asexual reproduction.

☐ identical   ☐ not identical

A mother pig feeds her piglets. Pigs reproduce using sexual reproduction.

☐ identical   ☐ not identical

Living Things Use Energy

Living things need energy to carry out the activities of life. Energy allows organisms to make or break down food, move materials into and out of cells, and build cells. Energy also allows organisms to move and interact with each other.

Where do living things get the energy they need for the activities of life? Plants convert energy from the sun into food. They store this food in their cells until they need to use it. Organisms that cannot make their own food must eat other organisms to gain energy. Some organisms eat plants. Others eat animals. Organisms such as fungi break down decaying material to gain energy.

10 Describe List three activities that you have done today that require energy.

_____

_____

_____

Living Things Grow and Mature

All living things grow during some period of their lives. When a unicellular organism grows, it gets larger and then divides, forming two cells. When a multicellular organism grows, the number of cells in its body increases, and the organism gets bigger.

Many living things don't just get larger as they grow. They also develop and change. Humans pass through different stages as they mature from childhood to adulthood. During these stages, the human body changes. Frogs and butterflies have body shapes that look completely different during different stages of development.

Visualize It!

11 Describe How does a frog grow and develop? Write a caption for each picture to describe each stage in a frog's life.

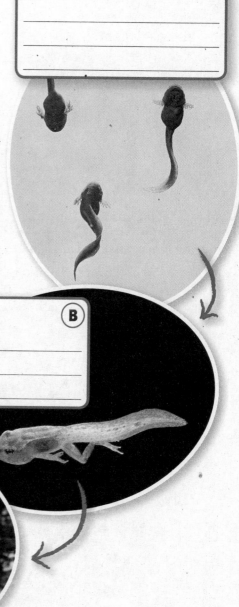

Younger Tadpoles (A)

_____

_____

Older Tadpole (B)

_____

_____

Adult Frog (C)

_____

_____

_____

Stayin' Alive

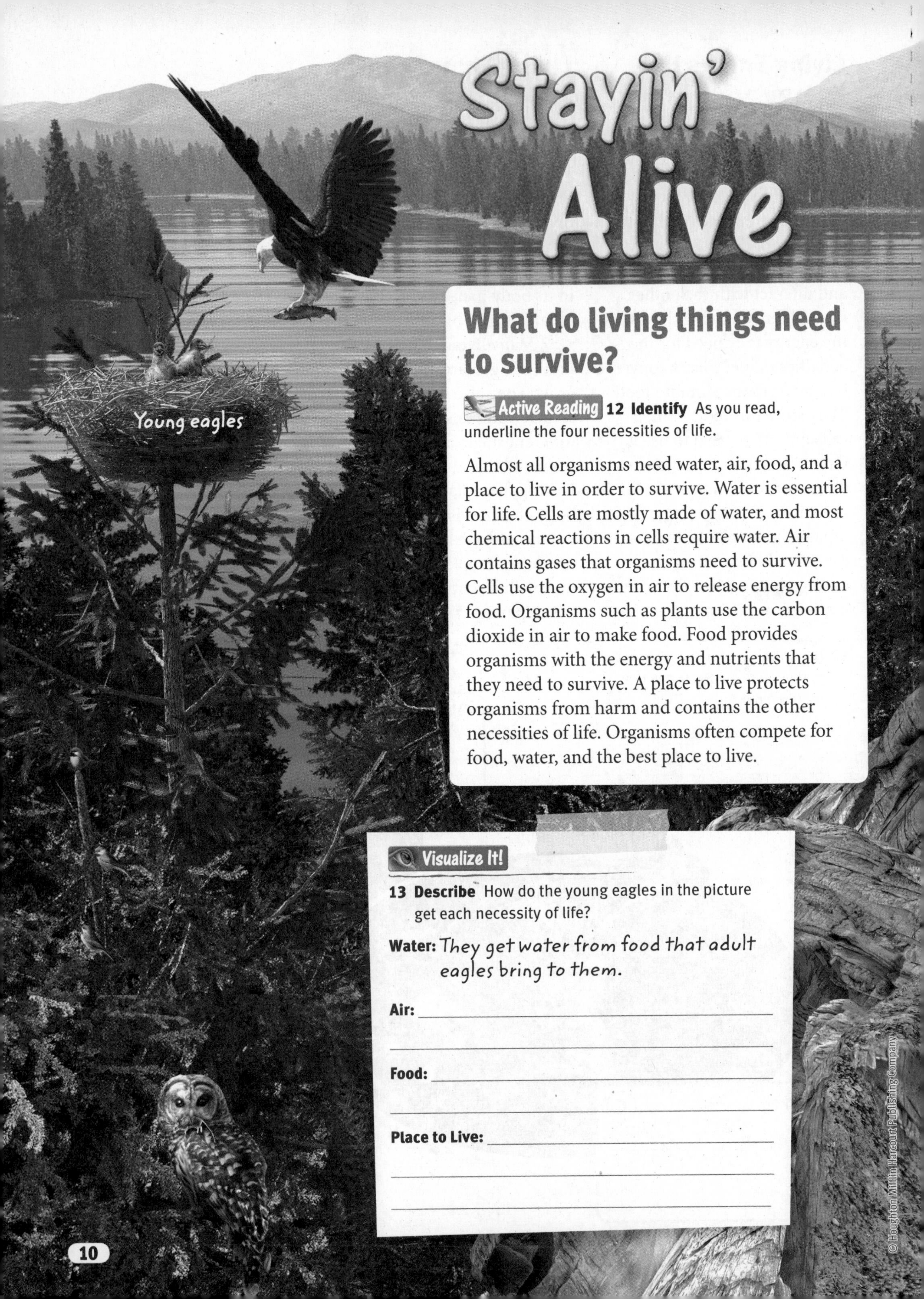

Young eagles

What do living things need to survive?

Active Reading **12 Identify** As you read, underline the four necessities of life.

Almost all organisms need water, air, food, and a place to live in order to survive. Water is essential for life. Cells are mostly made of water, and most chemical reactions in cells require water. Air contains gases that organisms need to survive. Cells use the oxygen in air to release energy from food. Organisms such as plants use the carbon dioxide in air to make food. Food provides organisms with the energy and nutrients that they need to survive. A place to live protects organisms from harm and contains the other necessities of life. Organisms often compete for food, water, and the best place to live.

Visualize It!

13 Describe How do the young eagles in the picture get each necessity of life?

Water: They get water from food that adult eagles bring to them.

Air: _____

_____

Food: _____

_____

Place to Live: _____

_____

_____

How do living things get food?

Food gives living things the energy and nutrients that they need to perform life processes. Nutrients include carbohydrates, lipids, and proteins. Fruits, vegetables, and grains provide carbohydrates. Nuts and fats provide lipids. Meats, nuts, and vegetables provide proteins.

Not all organisms get food in the same way. Producers make their own food. Consumers eat other organisms to get food. Decomposers break down dead organisms or wastes to get their food. Plants and algae are examples of producers. They use energy from the sun to make food. Animals such as deer are consumers that eat plants. Mice and squirrels are consumers that eat seeds from plants. Owls and eagles are consumers that eat other animals. Worms, bacteria, and fungi are examples of decomposers. They return nutrients to the soil, which other organisms can use.

Visualize It!

14 Describe Look for these four organisms in the picture. How does each organism get its food?

Organism	Classification	Way of Getting Food
Barred Owl	Consumer	Eats mice and other small animals
Earthworm		
Red Squirrel		
Fern		

Visual Summary

To complete this summary, circle the correct word. Then use the key below to check your answers. You can use this page to review the main concepts of the lesson.

Introduction to Living Things

All living things are made of cells that contain DNA. Living things use energy, grow and develop, and reproduce. They also respond to changes in their environment.

> **15** Sunlight is an example of (a) homeostasis / stimulus.
>
> **16** Binary fission is an example of asexual / sexual reproduction.

Almost all living things need water, air, food, and a place to live.

> **17** Plants are producers / consumers.
>
> **18** Decomposers return organisms / nutrients to the environment.

Answers: 15 stimulus; 16 asexual; 17 producers; 18 nutrients

19 Hypothesize How do some producers and consumers each rely on light from the sun?

Lesson Review

Vocabulary

In your own words, define the following terms.

1 homeostasis

_____

_____

2 asexual reproduction

_____

_____

3 cell

_____

_____

Key Concepts

4 Explain What is the relationship between a stimulus and a response?

_____

_____

_____

_____

5 Describe What happens to DNA during sexual reproduction?

_____

_____

_____

_____

6 Contrast What are the differences between producers, consumers, and decomposers?

_____

_____

_____

_____

Critical Thinking

Use the pictures to answer the questions below.

7 Describe What is happening to the birds in the picture above?

_____

_____

_____

_____

8 Explain How do nutrients and energy allow the changes shown in the picture to happen?

_____

_____

_____

_____

_____

_____

9 Compare How is a fish similar to an oak tree?

_____

_____

_____

_____

10 Making Inferences Could life as we know it exist on Earth if air contained only oxygen? Explain.

_____

_____

_____

_____

My Notes

Theory of Evolution by Natural Selection

ESSENTIAL QUESTION

What is the theory of evolution by natural selection?

By the end of this lesson, you should be able to describe the role of genetic and environmental factors in the theory of evolution by natural selection.

Because this grass snake's skin color looks like the plant stalk, it is able to hide from predators! This form of camouflage is the result of natural selection.

Lesson Labs

Quick Labs
• Model Natural Selection
• Analyzing Survival Adaptations
• The Opposable Thumb

Exploration Lab
• Environmental Change and Evolution

Engage Your Brain

1 Predict Check T or F to show whether you think each statement is true or false.

T F

☐ ☐ Fur color can help prevent an animal from being eaten.

☐ ☐ The amount of available food can affect an organism's survival.

☐ ☐ Your parents' characteristics are not passed on to you.

☐ ☐ A species can go extinct if its habitat is destroyed.

2 Infer How do you think this bird and this flower are related? Explain your answer.

_____

_____

_____

_____

Active Reading

3 Synthesize You can often define an unknown word by clues provided in the sentence. Use the sentence below to make an educated guess about the meaning of the word _artificial_.

Example sentence:
Many people prefer real sugar to artificial sweeteners made by humans.

artificial:

_____

_____

_____

Vocabulary Terms

• evolution
• artificial selection
• natural selection
• variation

• mutation
• adaptation
• extinction

4 Apply As you learn the definition of each vocabulary term in this lesson, create your own definition or sketch to help you remember the meaning of the term.

Darwin's Voyage

What did Darwin observe?

Charles Darwin was born in England in 1809. When he was 22 years old, Darwin graduated from college with a degree in theology. But he was also interested in plants and animals. Darwin became the naturalist—a scientist who studies nature—on the British ship HMS *Beagle*.

During his voyage, Darwin observed and collected many living and fossil specimens. He made some of his most important observations on the Galápagos Islands of South America. He kept a log that was later published as *The Voyage of the Beagle*. With the observations he made on this almost five-year journey, Darwin formed his idea about how biological evolution could happen.

In biology, **evolution** refers to the process by which populations change over time. A population is all of the individuals of a species that live in an area at the same time. A species is a group of closely related organisms that can mate to produce fertile offspring. Darwin developed a hypothesis, which eventually became a theory, of how evolution takes place.

Darwin left England on December 27, 1831. He returned 5 years later.

ENGLAND

EUROPE

NORTH AMERICA

ATLANTIC OCEAN

AFRICA

The plants and animals on the Galápagos Islands differed from island to island. This is where Darwin studied birds called finches.

Galápagos Islands

Equator

SOUTH AMERICA

Cape of Good Hope

Think Outside the Book Inquiry

5 Explore Trace Darwin's route on the map, and choose one of the following stops on his journey: Galápagos Islands, Andes Mountains, Australia. Do research to find out what plants and animals live there. Then write an entry in Darwin's log to describe what he might have seen.

Differences among Species

Darwin collected birds from the Galápagos Islands and nearby islands. He observed that these birds differed slightly from those on the nearby mainland of South America. And the birds on each island were different from the birds on the other islands. Careful analysis back in England revealed that they were all finches! Eventually, Darwin suggested that these birds may have evolved from one species of finch.

Darwin observed differences in beak size among finches from different islands. Many years later, scientists confirmed that these differences related to the birds' diets. Birds with shorter, heavier beaks could eat harder foods than those with thinner beaks.

This cactus finch has a narrow beak that it can use in many ways, including to pull grubs and insects from holes in the cactus.

This vegetarian finch has a curved beak, ideal for taking large berries from a branch.

ASIA

© Houghton Mifflin Harcourt Publishing Company •Image Credits: (t) ©blickwinkel/Alamy; (cl) ©Tim Graham/Alamy

Visualize It!

6 Infer How do you think the pointed beak of this woodpecker finch helps it to get food?

_____

_____

_____

Woodpecker finch

Equator

INDIAN OCEAN

AUSTRALIA

NEW ZEALAND

Darwin saw many plants and animals that were found only on certain continents such as Australia.

km 0   1,000   2,000

mi 0   1,000   2,000

Darwin's Homework

What other ideas influenced Darwin?

The ideas of many scientists and observations of the natural world influenced Darwin's thinking. Darwin drew on ideas about Earth's history, the growth of populations, and observations of how traits are passed on in selective breeding. All of these pieces helped him develop his ideas about how populations could change over time.

This chicken has been bred to have large tail feathers and a big red comb.

Organisms Pass Traits On to Offspring

Farmers and breeders have been producing many kinds of domestic animals and plants for thousands of years. These plants and animals have traits that the farmers and breeders desire. A *trait* is a form of an inherited characteristic. For example, the length of tail feathers is an inherited characteristic, and short or long tail feathers are the corresponding traits. The practice by which humans select plants or animals for breeding based on desired traits is **artificial selection**. Artificial selection shows that traits can change. Traits can also spread through populations.

This chicken has been bred to have large head feathers.

---

7 List Darwin studied artificial selection in the pigeons that he bred. List three other domestic animals that have many different breeds.

_____

_____

_____

_____

This chicken has been bred to have feathers on its feet.

8 Identify As you read, underline the names of other important thinkers who influenced Darwin's ideas.

Organisms Acquire Traits

Scientist Jean-Baptiste Lamarck thought that organisms could acquire and pass on traits they needed to survive. For example, a man could develop stronger muscles over time. If the muscles were an advantage in his environment, Lamarck thought the man would pass on this trait to his offspring. Now we know that acquired traits are not passed on to offspring because these traits do not become part of an organism's DNA. But the fact that species change, and the idea that an organism's traits help it survive, shaped Darwin's ideas.

9 Apply Explain why the size of your muscles is partly an acquired trait and partly dependent on DNA.

_____

_____

_____

_____

These rock layers formed over millions of years.

Earth Changes over Time

The presence of different rock layers, such as those in the photo, show that Earth has changed over time. Geologist Charles Lyell hypothesized that small changes in rock have collected over hundreds of millions of years. Darwin reasoned that if Earth were very old, then there would be enough time for very small changes in life forms to add up.

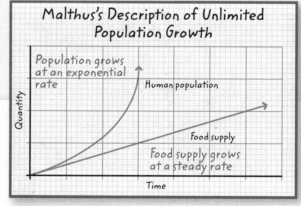

Malthus's Description of Unlimited Population Growth

Population grows at an exponential rate

Human population

Food supply

Food supply grows at a steady rate

Quantity

Time

A Struggle for Survival Exists

After his journey, Darwin read an essay about population growth by economist Thomas Malthus. The essay helped Darwin understand how the environment could influence which organisms survive and which organisms die. All populations are affected by factors that limit population growth, such as disease, predation, and competition for food. Darwin reasoned that the survivors probably have traits that help them survive and that some of these traits could be passed on from parent to offspring.

10 Summarize What can you conclude from the two red growth lines on this graph?

_____

_____

_____

Natural Selection

What are the four parts of natural selection?

Darwin proposed that most evolution happens through the natural selection of advantageous traits. **Natural selection** is the process by which organisms that inherit advantageous traits tend to reproduce more successfully than other organisms do.

Overproduction

When a plant or animal reproduces, it usually makes more offspring than the environment can support. For example, a female jaguar may have up to four pups at a time. Only some of them will survive to adulthood, and a smaller number of them will successfully reproduce.

11 **Infer** A fish may have hundreds of offspring at a time, and only a small number will survive. Which characteristics of fish might allow them to survive?

_____

_____

_____

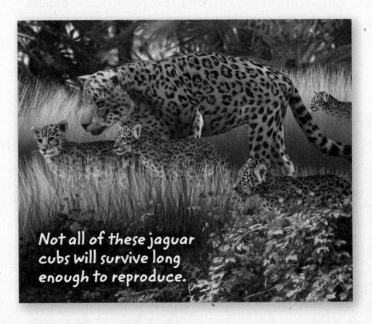

Not all of these jaguar cubs will survive long enough to reproduce.

Variation exists in the jaw sizes of these two jaguars. This variation will be passed on to the next generation.

Genetic Variation

Within a species there are naturally occurring differences, or **variations**, in traits. For example, in the two jaguar skulls to the left, one jaw is larger than the other. This difference results from a difference in the genetic material of the jaguars. Genetic variations can be passed on from parent to offspring. An important source of variation is a **mutation**, or change in genetic material.

As each new generation is produced, genetic variation may be introduced into a population. The more genetic variation in a population, the more likely it is that some individuals might have traits that will be advantageous if the environment changes. Also, genetic variation can lead to diversity of organisms as a population adapts to changing environments.

© Houghton Mifflin Harcourt Publishing Company

Selection

Individuals try to get the resources they need to survive. These resources include food, water, space and, in most cases, mates for reproduction. About 11,000 years ago, jaguars faced a shortage of food because the climate changed and many prey species died out. A genetic variation in jaw size then became important for survival. Jaguars with larger jaws could eat hard-shelled reptiles when other prey were hard to find.

Darwin reasoned that individuals with a particular trait, such as a large jaw, are more likely to survive long enough to reproduce. As a result, the trait is "selected" for, becoming more common in the next generation of offspring.

12 Summarize How did large jaws and teeth become typical traits of jaguars?

_____

_____

_____

A larger jaw makes it easier for this jaguar to eat hard-shelled turtles.

Adaptation

An inherited trait that helps an organism survive and reproduce in its environment is an **adaptation**. Adaptation is the selection of naturally occurring trait variations in populations. Jaguars with larger jaws were able to survive and reproduce when food was hard to find. As natural selection continues, adaptations grow more common in the population with each new generation. Over time, the population becomes better adapted to the environment.

Large jaw size is one adaptation of jaguars.

13 Explain In the table below, explain how each part of natural selection works.

Principle of natural selection	How it works
overproduction	
genetic variation	
selection	
adaptation	

Well-adapted

How do species change over time?

In order for a population to change, some individuals have to be different from other members of the population. Mutations are one of the main sources of genetic variation. Offspring sometimes inherit a gene that has a slight mutation, or change, from the gene the parent has. Mutations can be harmful, helpful, or have no effect. Beneficial mutations help individuals survive and reproduce.

Over Generations, Adaptations Become More Common

Active Reading **14 Identify** Underline examples of adaptations.

Adaptations are inherited traits that help organisms survive and reproduce. Some adaptations, such as a duck's webbed feet, are internal or external structures. Other adaptations are inherited behaviors that help an organism find food, protect itself, or reproduce. At first, an adaptation is rare in a population. Imagine a bird population in which some birds have short beaks. If more birds with shorter beaks survive and reproduce than birds with longer beaks, more birds in the next generation will probably have short beaks. The number of individuals with the adaptation would continue to increase.

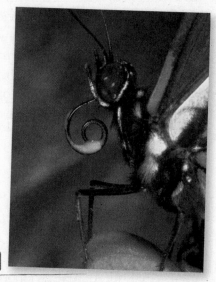

Visualize It!

15 Write a caption to describe how this butterfly's long mouth part helps it to survive.

_____

_____

_____

_____

Genetic Differences Add Up

Parents and offspring often have small differences in genetic material. Over many generations, the small differences can add up. These differences accumulate so that organisms alive now are often very different from their ancestors. As a result, there is great diversity among organisms. For example, the antibiotic penicillin was able to kill many types of bacteria in the 1950s. Today, some of those species of bacteria are now completely resistant to penicillin. The genetic makeup of these bacterial populations has changed. New fossil discoveries and new information about genes add to scientists' understanding of natural selection and evolution.

The male frigate bird uses his red throat pouch to attract a female, which could lead to reproduction.

What happens to species as the environment changes?

Certain environments favor certain traits. Consider a snake population with either brown- or green-colored snakes. In a forest that has many dead leaves on the ground, brown snakes will blend in better than green snakes will. But in an area with more grass, the green snakes may be better at hiding from predators. Changes in environmental conditions can affect the survival of organisms with a particular trait. Environmental changes can also lead to diversity of organisms by increasing the number of species.

Dinosaurs went extinct 65 million years ago.

Adaptations Can Allow a Species to Survive

All organisms have traits that allow them to survive in specific environments. For example, plants have xylem tissue that carries water up from the roots to the rest of the plant.

If the environment changes, a species is more likely to survive if it has genetic variation. For example, imagine a species of grass in which some plants need less water than others. If the environment became drier, many grass plants would die, but the plants that needed less water might survive. These plants might eventually become a new species if they cannot reproduce with the plants that needed more water.

Some Species May Become Extinct

If no individuals have traits that help them to survive and reproduce in the changed environment, a species will become extinct. **Extinction** occurs when all members of a species have died. Greater competition, new predators, and the loss of habitat are examples of environmental changes that can lead to extinction. Some extinctions are caused by natural disasters. Because a natural disaster can destroy resources quickly, organisms may die no matter what adaptations they have. The fossil record shows that many species have become extinct in the history of life on Earth.

Visualize It!

Environmental change has affected the environmental conditions near the North Pole.

16 Summarize How has ice cover near the North Pole changed in the last few decades?

_____

_____

17 Infer How do you think this environmental change will affect species that live in the surrounding area?

_____

_____

_____

_____

Bering Sea

km 0   300   600
mi 0   300   600

ASIA

Minimum ice cover
- 1979–2000 median
- 2005
- 2007

+ North Pole

Barents Sea

EUROPE

NORTH AMERICA

Baffin Bay

Norwegian Sea

Source: National Aeronautics and Space Administration, 2007

Visual Summary

To complete this summary, circle the correct word. Then use the key below to check your answers. You can use this page to review the main concepts of the lesson.

Evolution is Change over Time

Darwin's theory of natural selection was influenced by his own observations and the work of other scientists.

18 Through natural / artificial selection, breeders choose the traits that are passed on to the next generation.

The theory of evolution by natural selection states that organisms with advantageous traits produce more offspring.

Many extinctions have occurred over the course of Earth's history.

20 Because of environmental change, dinosaurs eventually became mutated / extinct.

19 Natural selection can act only on acquired traits / inherited variation.

Answers: 18 artificial, 19 inherited variation, 20 extinct

21 Infer How does the environment influence natural selection?

Lesson Review

Vocabulary

Use a term from the lesson to complete the sentences below.

1 The four parts of natural selection are overproduction, _____, selection, and adaptation.

2 _____ is the process by which populations change over time.

3 The hollow bones of birds, which keep birds lightweight for flying, is an example of a(n) _____

Key Concepts

4 Summarize Describe Darwin's observations on the Galápagos islands during his voyage on the HMS *Beagle*.

_____

_____

_____

_____

5 Explain How does environmental change affect the survival of a species?

_____

_____

_____

_____

6 Compare Why are only inherited traits, not acquired ones, involved in the process of natural selection?

_____

_____

_____

7 Describe What is the relationship between mutation, natural selection, and adaptation?

_____

_____

_____

_____

Critical Thinking

Use the diagram to answer the following question.

8 Apply How is each of these lizards adapted to its environment?

_____

_____

_____

_____

_____

_____

_____

_____

9 Infer What might happen to a population of rabbits in a forest if a new predator moved to the forest?

_____

_____

_____

_____

_____

_____

My Notes

Scientific Debate

Not all scientific knowledge is gained through experimentation.
It is also the result of a great deal of debate and confirmation.

Tutorial

As you prepare for a debate, look for information from the following sources.

Controlled Experiments Consider the following points when planning or examining the results of a controlled experiment.

- Only one factor should be tested at a time. A factor is anything in the experiment that can influence the outcome.
- Samples are divided into experimental group(s) and a control group. All of the factors of the experimental group(s) and the control group are the same except for one variable.
- A variable is a factor that can be changed. If there are multiple variables, only one variable should be changed at a time.

Independent Studies The results of a different group may provide stronger support for your argument than your own results. And using someone else's results helps to avoid the claim that your results are biased. Bias is the tendency to think about something from only one point of view. The claim of bias can be used to argue against your point.

Comparison with Similar Objects or Events If you cannot gather data from an experiment to help support your position, finding a similar object or event might help. The better your example is understood, the stronger your argument will be.

Read the passage below and answer the questions.

Many people want to protect endangered species but do not agree on the best methods to use. Incubating, or heating eggs to ensure hatching, is commonly used with bird eggs. It was logical to apply the same technique to turtle eggs. The Barbour's map turtle is found in Florida, Georgia, and Alabama. To help more turtles hatch, people would gather eggs and incubate them. However, debate really began when mostly female turtles hatched. Were efforts to help the turtles really harming them? Scientists learned that incubating eggs at 25°C (77°F) produces males and at 30°C (86°F) produces females. As a result, conservation programs have stopped artificially heating the eggs.

1 What is the variable described in the article about Barbour's map turtles?

_____

2 Write a list of factors that were likely kept the same between the sample groups described in the article.

_____

_____

_____

3 What argument could people have used who first suggested incubating the turtle eggs?

_____

_____

_____

You Try It!

Fossils from the Burgess Shale Formation in Canada include many strange creatures that lived over 500 million years ago. The fossils are special because the soft parts of the creatures were preserved. Examine the fossil of the creature *Marrella* and the reconstruction of what it might have looked like.

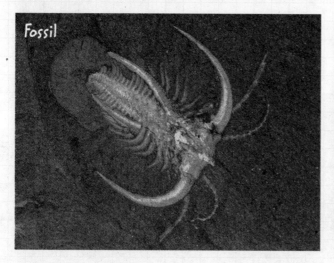

Fossil

Reconstruction

1 Recognizing Relationships Find four features on the reconstruction that you can also identify in the fossil. Write a brief description of each feature.

_____
_____
_____
_____
_____
_____
_____

2 Applying Concepts *Marrella* is extinct. How do you think *Marrella* behaved when it was alive? What did it eat? How did it move? On what do you base your argument?

_____
_____
_____
_____
_____
_____
_____
_____

3 Communicating Ideas Share your description with a classmate. Discuss and debate your positions. Complete the table to show the points on which you agree and disagree.

Agree	Disagree

Take It Home

Research more about the creatures of the Burgess Shale Formation. Find at least one other fossil creature and its reconstruction. What do you think the creature was like?

Evidence of Evolution

ESSENTIAL QUESTION

What evidence supports the theory of evolution?

By the end of this lesson, you should be able to describe the evidence that supports the theory of evolution by natural selection.

Fossils show us what a dinosaur looks like. This dinosaur lived millions of years ago!

© Houghton Mifflin Harcourt Publishing Company • Image Credits: ©Bill Varie/Corbis

Lesson Labs

Quick Labs
• Comparing Anatomy
• Genetic Evidence for Evolution

Field Lab
• Mystery Footprints

 Engage Your Brain

1 Predict Check T or F to show whether you think each statement is true or false.

T	F	
☐	☐	Fossils provide evidence of organisms that lived in the past.
☐	☐	The wing of a bat has similar bones to those in a human arm.
☐	☐	DNA can tell us how closely related two organisms are.
☐	☐	Whales are descended from land-dwelling mammals.

2 Infer This is a Petoskey stone, which is made up of tiny coral fossils. What can you infer if you find a coral fossil on land?

Petoskey stone

_____
_____
_____
_____

 Active Reading

3 Synthesize You can often define an unknown word if you understand the parts of the word. Use the words below to make an educated guess about the meaning of the word *fossil record*.

Word	Meaning
fossil	the remains or trace of once-living organisms
record	an account that preserves information about facts or events

Vocabulary Terms

• fossil   • fossil record

4 Apply As you learn the definition of each vocabulary term in this lesson, create your own definition or sketch to help you remember the meaning of the term.

fossil record:

_____
_____
_____

Fossil Hunt

How do fossils form?

Evidence that organisms have changed over time can be found in amber, ice, or sedimentary rock. Sedimentary rock is formed when particles of sand or soil are deposited in horizontal layers. Often this occurs as mud or silt hardens. After one rock layer forms, newer rock layers form on top of it. So, older layers are found below or underneath younger rock layers. The most basic principle of dating such rocks and the remains of organisms inside is "the deeper it is, the older it is."

Amber fossils form when small creatures are trapped in tree sap and the sap hardens.

5 Examine What features of the organism are preserved in amber?

_____

_____

_____

This flying dinosaur is an example of a cast fossil.

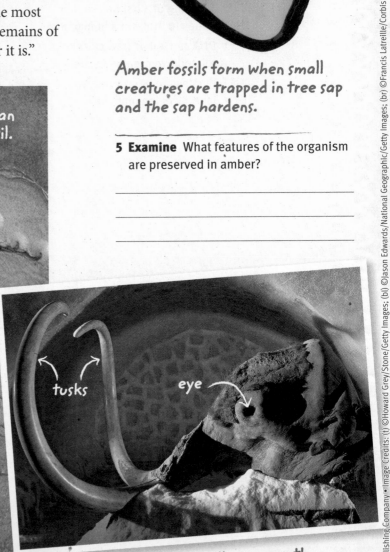

tusks

eye

Because this woolly mammoth was frozen in ice, its skin and hair were preserved.

© Houghton Mifflin Harcourt Publishing Company • Image Credits: (t) ©Howard Grey/Stone/Getty Images; (bl) ©Jason Edwards/National Geographic/Getty Images; (br) ©Francis Latreille/Corbis

Many Fossils Form in Sedimentary Rock

Rock layers preserve evidence of organisms that were once alive. The remains or imprints of once-living organisms are called **fossils**. Fossils commonly form when a dead organism is covered by a layer of sediment or mud. Over time, more sediment settles on top of the organism. Minerals in the sediment may seep into the organism and replace the body's material with minerals that harden over time. This process produces a cast fossil. Many familiar fossils are casts of hard parts, such as shells and bones. If the organism rots away completely after being covered, it may leave an imprint of itself in the rock. Despite all of the fossils that have been found, it is rare for an organism to become a fossil. Most often, the dead organism is recycled back into the biological world by scavengers, decomposers, or the process of weathering.

Active Reading

6 Identify As you read, underline the steps that describe how a cast fossil forms.

How do fossils show change over time?

All of the fossils that have been discovered make up the **fossil record**. The fossil record provides evidence about the order in which species have existed through time, and how they have changed over time. By examining the fossil record, scientists can learn about the history of life on Earth.

Despite all the fossils that have been found, there are gaps in the fossil record. These gaps represent chunks of geologic time for which a fossil has not been discovered. Also, the transition between two groups of organisms may not be well understood. Fossils that help fill in these gaps are *transitional fossils*. The illustration on the right is based on a transitional fossil.

Fossils found in newer layers of Earth's crust tend to have physical or molecular similarities to present-day organisms. These similarities indicate that the fossilized organisms were close relatives of the present-day organisms. Fossils from older layers are less similar to present-day organisms than fossils from newer layers are. Most older fossils are of earlier life-forms such as dinosaurs, which don't exist anymore.

Visualize It!

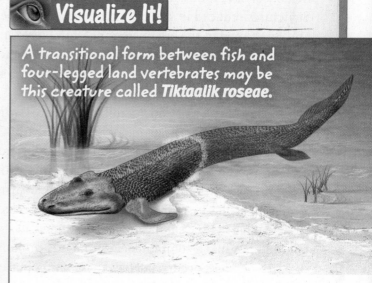

A transitional form between fish and four-legged land vertebrates may be this creature called *Tiktaalik roseae.*

7 Identify Describe the environment in which this organism lives.

_____

_____

8 Infer How is this organism like both a fish and a four-legged vertebrate, such as an amphibian?

_____

_____

_____

More clues . . .

What other evidence supports evolution?

Many fields of study provide evidence that modern species and extinct species share an ancestor. A *common ancestor* is the most recent species from which two different species have evolved. Structural data, DNA, developmental patterns, and fossils all support the theory that populations change over time. Sometimes these populations become new species. Biologists observe that all living organisms have some traits in common and inherit traits in similar ways. Evidence of when and where those ancestors lived and what they looked like is found in the fossil record.

Active Reading

9 List What is a common ancestor?

_____

_____

_____

Common Structures

Scientists have found that related organisms share structural traits. Structures reduced in size or function may have been complete and functional in the organism's ancestor. For example, snakes have traces of leglike structures that are not used for movement. These unused structures are evidence that snakes share a common ancestor with animals like lizards and dogs.

Scientists also consider similar structures with different functions. The arm of a human, the front leg of a cat, and the wing of a bat do not look alike and are not used in the same way. But as you can see, they are similar in structure. The bones of a human arm are similar in structure to the bones in the front limbs of a cat and a bat. These similarities suggest that cats, bats, and humans had a common ancestor. Over millions of years, changes occurred. Now, these bones perform different functions in each type of animal.

front limb of a bat

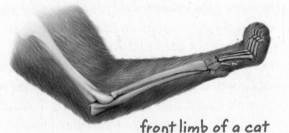

front limb of a cat

Visualize It!

10 Relate Do you see any similarities between the bones of the bat and cat limbs and the bones of the human arm? If so, use the colors of the bat and cat bones to color similar bones in the human arm. If you don't have colored pencils, label the bones with the correct color names.

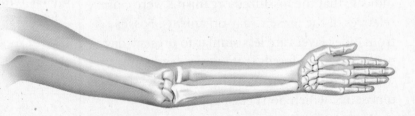

Similar DNA

The genetic information stored in an organism's DNA determines the organism's traits. Because an organism's DNA stays almost exactly the same throughout its entire lifetime, scientists can compare the DNA from many organisms. The greater the number of similarities between the molecules of any two species, the more recently the two species most likely shared a common ancestor.

Recall that DNA determines which amino acids make up a protein. Scientists have compared the amino acids that make up cytochrome c proteins in many species. Cytochrome c is involved in cellular respiration. Organisms that have fewer amino acid differences are more likely to be closely related.

Frogs also have cytochrome c proteins, but they're a little different from yours.

Cytochrome C Comparison	
Organism	Number of amino acid differences from human cytochrome c
Chimpanzee	0
Rhesus monkey	1
Whale	10
Turtle	15
Bullfrog	18
Lamprey	20

Source: M.Dayhoff, *Atlas of Protein Sequence and Structure*

Visualize It!

11 Infer The number of amino acids in human cytochrome c differs between humans and the species at left. Which two species do you infer are the least closely related to humans?

_____

_____

_____

_____

Developmental Similarities

The study of development is called *embryology*. Embryos undergo many physical and functional changes as they grow and develop. If organisms develop in similar ways, they also likely share a common ancestor.

Scientists have compared the development of different species to look for similar patterns and structures. Scientists think that such similarities come from an ancestor that the species have in common. For example, at some time during development, all animals with backbones have a tail. This observation suggests that they shared a common ancestor.

These embryos are at a similar stage of development.

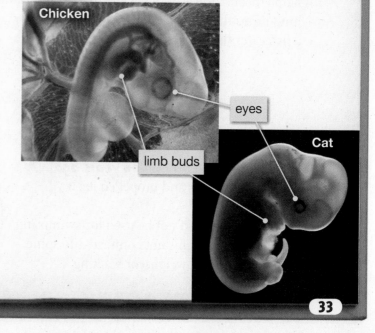

Chicken

eyes

Cat

limb buds

How do we know organisms are related?

Scientists examine organisms carefully for clues about their ancestors. In a well-studied example, scientists looked at the characteristics of whales that made them different from other ocean animals. Unlike fish and sharks, whales breathe air, give birth to live young, and produce milk. Fossil and DNA evidence support the hypothesis that modern whales evolved from hoofed mammals that lived on land.

Fossil Evidence

Scientists have examined fossils of extinct species that have features in between whales and land mammals. These features are called *transitional characters*. None of these species are directly related to modern whales. But their skeletons suggest how a gradual transition from land mammal to aquatic whale could have happened.

Ⓐ *Pakicetus*   52 million years ago
- whale-shaped skull and teeth adapted for hunting fish
- ran on four legs
- ear bones in between those of land and aquatic mammals

Ⓑ *Ambulocetus natans*   50 million years ago
- name means "the walking whale that swims"
- hind limbs that were adapted for swimming
- a fish eater that lived on water and on land

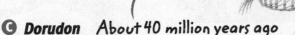

Ⓒ *Dorudon*   About 40 million years ago
- lived in warm seas and propelled itself with a long tail
- tiny hind legs could not be used for swimming
- pelvis and hind limbs not connected to spine, could not support weight for walking

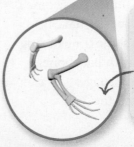

Unused Structures
Most modern whales have pelvic bones and some have leg bones. These bones do not help the animal move.

Molecular Evidence

The DNA of whales is very similar to the DNA of hoofed mammals. Below are some DNA fragments of a gene that makes a type of milk protein.

Hippopotamus   TCC TGGCA GTCCA GTGGT

Humpback whale CCC TGGCA GTGCA GTGCT

12 Identify Circle the pairs of nitrogen bases (G, T, C, or A) that differ between the hippopotamus and humpback whale DNA.

13 Infer How do you think these bones are involved in a whale's movement?

_____

_____

_____

Modern Whale   *Present day*

• no hind limbs, front limbs are flippers
• some whales have tiny hip bones left over from their hoofed-mammal ancestors
• breathe air with lungs like other mammals do

14 Analyze Examine the four skeletons. Indicate which species appears to be best adapted for swimming underwater for a long time. Which characters allow the animal to behave this way?

_____

_____

_____

_____

_____

_____

Visual Summary

To complete this summary, circle the correct word. Then use the key below to check your answers. You can use this page to review the main concepts of the lesson.

Evidence of Evolution

Fossil evidence shows that life on Earth has changed over time.

15 The remains of once-living organisms are called fossils / ancestors.

Scientists use evidence from many fields of research to study the common ancestors of living organisms.

Evolutionary theory is also supported by structural, genetic, and developmental evidence.

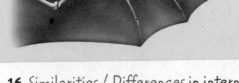

16 Similarities / Differences in internal structures support evidence of common ancestry.

17 The tiny leg bones / large dorsal fins of modern whales are an example of unused structures.

Answers: 15 fossils, 16 similarities, 17 tiny leg bones

18 Summarize How does the fossil record provide evidence of the diversity of life?

Lesson Review

Vocabulary

1 Which word means "the remains or imprints of once-living organisms found in layers of rock?"

_____

2 Which word means "the history of life in the geologic past as indicated by the imprints or remains of living things?"

_____

Key Concepts

3 Identify What are two types of evidence that suggest that evolution has occurred?

_____
_____
_____

4 Explain How do fossils provide evidence that evolution has taken place?

_____
_____
_____

5 Apply What is the significance of the similar number and arrangement of bones in a human arm and a bat wing?

_____
_____
_____

Critical Thinking

6 Imagine If you were a scientist examining the DNA sequence of two unknown organisms that you hypothesize share a common ancestor, what evidence would you expect to find?

_____
_____
_____

Use this table to answer the following questions.

Cytochrome C Comparison	
Organism	Number of amino acid differences from human cytochrome c
Chimpanzee	0
Turtle	15
Tuna	21

Source: M. Dayhoff, *Atlas of Protein Sequence and Structure*

7 Identify What do the data suggest about how related turtles are to humans compared to tuna and chimpanzees?

_____
_____
_____

8 Infer If there are no differences between the amino acid sequences in the cytochrome c protein of humans and chimpanzees, why aren't we the same species?

_____
_____
_____

9 Apply Explain why the pattern of differences that exists from earlier to later fossils in the fossil record supports the idea that evolution has taken place on Earth.

_____
_____
_____
_____

My Notes

The History of Life on Earth

ESSENTIAL QUESTION

How has life on Earth changed over time?

By the end of this lesson, you should be able to describe the evolution of life on Earth over time, using the geologic time scale.

Trilobites like this one lived on Earth about 400 million years ago. This fossil preserved great detail of the trilobite's body parts.

Lesson Labs

Quick Labs
- How Do We Know What Happened When?
- Investigate Relative and Absolute Age

Engage Your Brain

1 Predict Check T or F to show whether you think each statement is true or false.

T	F	
☐	☐	A mass extinction occurs when a large number of species go extinct during a relatively short amount of time.
☐	☐	The largest division of the geologic time scale is the era.
☐	☐	We currently live in the Cenozoic era.
☐	☐	Fossils show that the first living things were very tiny.

2 Draw Imagine you find a fossil of a fish. Which parts of the fish could you see in the fossil? Draw what you think you would see below.

Active Reading

3 Apply Use context clues to write your own definition for the words *fossil record* and *extinction.*

Example sentence
Scientists develop hypotheses about Earth's history based on observable changes in the fossil record.

fossil record:

____

____

Example sentence
Endangered species are protected by law in an effort to preserve them from extinction.

extinction:

____

____

Vocabulary Terms

- fossil
- extinction
- fossil record
- geologic time scale

4 Identify As you read, place a question mark next to any words that you don't understand. When you finish reading the lesson, go back and review the text that you marked. If the information is still confusing, consult a classmate or a teacher.

Uncovering Clues

How do we learn about ancient life?

Paleontologists look for clues to understand what happened in the past. These scientists use fossils to reconstruct the history of life. A **fossil** is a trace or imprint of a living thing that is preserved by geological processes. Fossils of single-celled organisms date as far back as 3.8 billion years.

What can we learn from fossils?

All of the fossils that have been discovered worldwide make up the **fossil record**. By examining the fossil record, scientists can identify when different species lived and died. There are two ways to describe the ages of fossils. *Relative dating* determines whether a fossil formed before or after another fossil. When an organism is trapped in mud or sediment, the resulting fossil becomes part of that sedimentary layer of rock. In rock layers that are not disturbed, newer fossils are found in layers of rock that are above older fossils. *Absolute dating* estimates the age of a fossil in years. Estimations are based on information from radioactive elements in certain rocks near the fossil.

Visualize It!

The abbreviation Ma stands for mega annum. A mega annum is equal to 1 million years. Ma is often used to indicate "million years ago."

5 Infer What does relative dating tell you about fossil A?

_____

_____

_____

6 Solve What does absolute dating tell you about fossil A?

_____

_____

_____

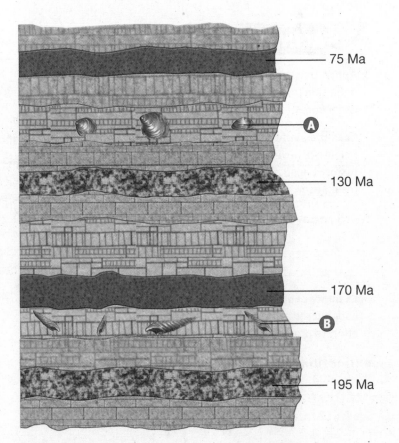

75 Ma

A

130 Ma

170 Ma

B

195 Ma

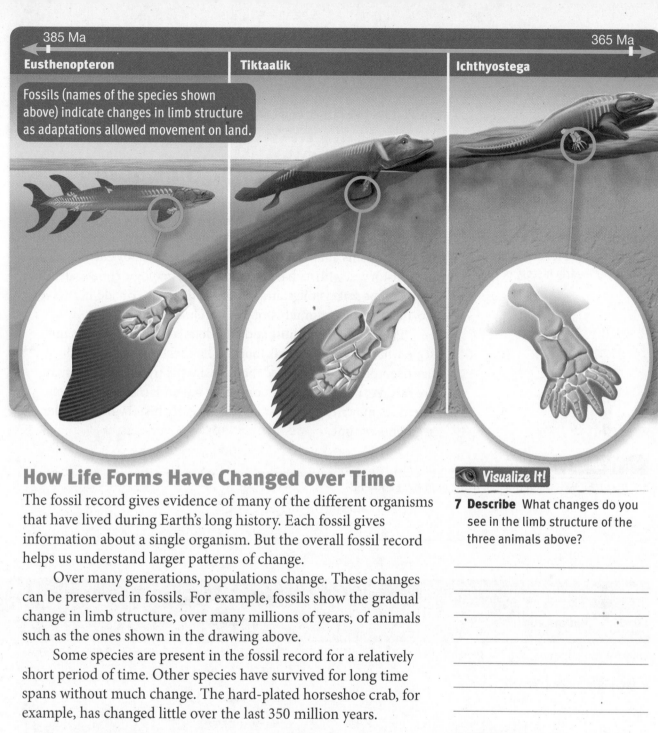

385 Ma   365 Ma

Eusthenopteron   **Tiktaalik**   **Ichthyostega**

Fossils (names of the species shown above) indicate changes in limb structure as adaptations allowed movement on land.

How Life Forms Have Changed over Time

The fossil record gives evidence of many of the different organisms that have lived during Earth's long history. Each fossil gives information about a single organism. But the overall fossil record helps us understand larger patterns of change.

Over many generations, populations change. These changes can be preserved in fossils. For example, fossils show the gradual change in limb structure, over many millions of years, of animals such as the ones shown in the drawing above.

Some species are present in the fossil record for a relatively short period of time. Other species have survived for long time spans without much change. The hard-plated horseshoe crab, for example, has changed little over the last 350 million years.

When Extinctions Occurred

An **extinction** happens when every individual of a species dies. A mass extinction occurs when a large number of species go extinct during a relatively short amount of time. Gradual environmental changes can cause mass extinctions. Catastrophic events, such as the impact of an asteroid, can also cause mass extinctions.

Extinctions and mass extinctions are documented in the fossil record. Fossils that were common in certain rock layers may decrease in frequency and eventually disappear altogether. Based on evidence in the fossil record, scientists form hypotheses about how and when species went extinct.

Visualize It!

7 Describe What changes do you see in the limb structure of the three animals above?

_____

_____

_____

_____

_____

_____

_____

Active Reading

8 Describe How can the extinction of an organism be inferred from evidence in the fossil record?

_____

_____

_____

_____

© Houghton Mifflin Harcourt Publishing Company

Way Back When

What is the geologic time scale?

After a fossil is dated, a paleontologist can place the fossil in chronological order with other fossils. This ordering allows scientists to hypothesize about relationships between species and how organisms changed over time. To keep track of Earth's long history, scientists have developed the geologic time scale. The **geologic time scale** is the standard method used to divide Earth's long 4.6-billion-year natural history into manageable parts.

Paleontologists adjust and add details to the geologic time scale when new evidence is found. The early history of Earth has been poorly understood, because fossils from this time span are rare. As new evidence about early life on Earth accumulates, scientists may need to organize Earth's early history into smaller segments of time.

Active Reading

9 Identify Underline one reason why it is hard for scientists to study the early history of Earth.

Visualize It!

10 Identify When did the Paleozoic era begin and end?

_____

_____

_____

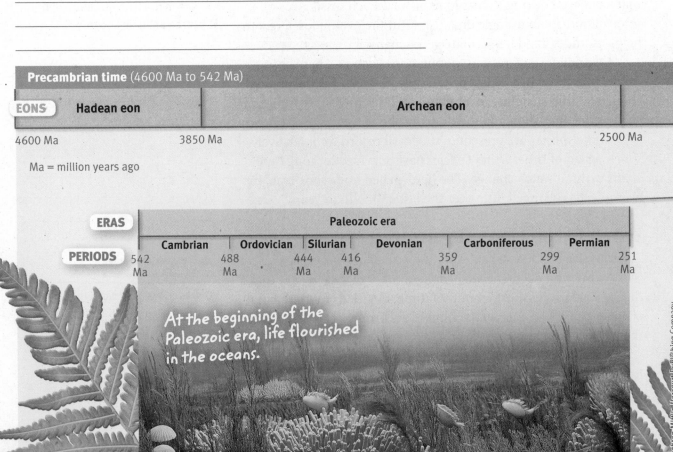

Precambrian time (4600 Ma to 542 Ma)		
EONS Hadean eon	Archean eon	
4600 Ma 3850 Ma	2500 Ma	

Ma = million years ago

ERAS			Paleozoic era				
PERIODS	Cambrian	Ordovician	Silurian	Devonian	Carboniferous	Permian	
	542 Ma	488 Ma	444 Ma	416 Ma	359 Ma	299 Ma	251 Ma

At the beginning of the Paleozoic era, life flourished in the oceans.

A Tool to Organize Earth's History

Boundaries between geologic time intervals correspond to significant changes in Earth's history. Some major boundaries are defined by mass extinctions or significant changes in the number of species. Other boundaries are defined by major changes in Earth's surface or climate.

The largest divisions of the geologic time scale are eons. Eons are divided into eras. Eras are characterized by the type of organism that dominated Earth at the time. Each era began with a change in the type of organism that was most dominant. Eras are further divided into periods, and periods are divided into epochs.

The four major divisions that make up the history of life on Earth are Precambrian time, the Paleozoic era, the Mesozoic era, and the Cenozoic era. Precambrian time is made up of the first three eons of Earth's history.

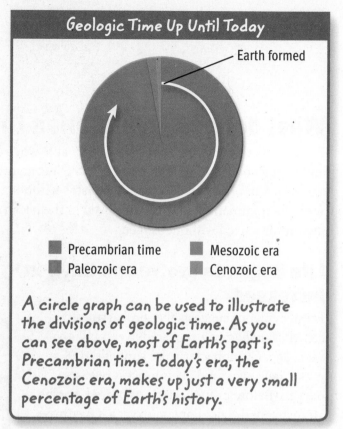

Geologic Time Up Until Today

Earth formed

■ Precambrian time
■ Paleozoic era
■ Mesozoic era
■ Cenozoic era

A circle graph can be used to illustrate the divisions of geologic time. As you can see above, most of Earth's past is Precambrian time. Today's era, the Cenozoic era, makes up just a very small percentage of Earth's history.

Visualize It!

11 List Which three periods make up the Mesozoic era?

_____

_____

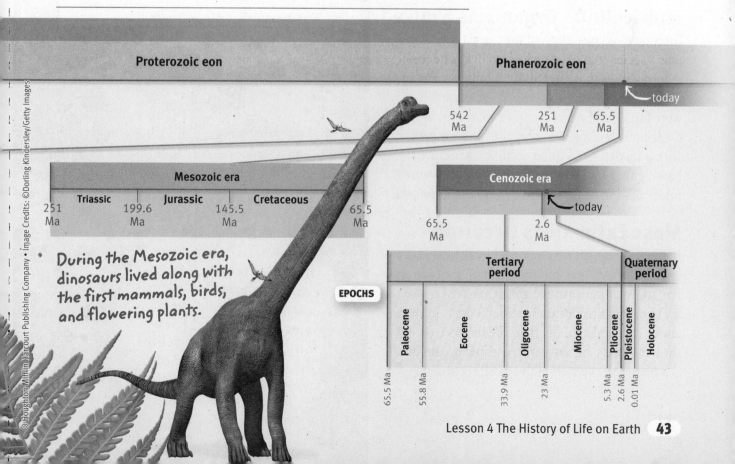

Proterozoic eon

Phanerozoic eon

today

542 Ma   251 Ma   65.5 Ma

Mesozoic era

| Triassic | Jurassic | Cretaceous |

251 Ma   199.6 Ma   145.5 Ma   65.5 Ma

During the Mesozoic era, dinosaurs lived along with the first mammals, birds, and flowering plants.

Cenozoic era

today

65.5 Ma   2.6 Ma

| Tertiary period | Quaternary period |

EPOCHS

Paleocene   Eocene   Oligocene   Miocene   Pliocene   Pleistocene   Holocene

65.5 Ma   55.8 Ma   33.9 Ma   23 Ma   5.3 Ma   2.6 Ma   0.01 Ma

Ancient Wisdom

What defined Precambrian time?

Precambrian time started 4.6 billion years ago, when Earth formed, and ended about 542 million years ago. Life began during this time. *Prokaryotes*—single-celled organisms without a nucleus—were the dominant life form. They lived in the ocean. The earliest prokaryotes lived without oxygen.

Life Began to Evolve and Oxygen Increased

Fossil evidence suggests that prokaryotes called *cyanobacteria* appeared over 3 billion years ago. Cyanobacteria use sunlight to make their own food. This process releases oxygen. Before cyanobacteria appeared, Earth's atmosphere did not contain oxygen. Over time, oxygen built up in the ocean and air. Eventually, the oxygen also formed *ozone,* a gas layer in the upper atmosphere. Ozone absorbs harmful radiation from the sun. Before ozone formed, life existed only in the oceans and underground.

Multicellular Organisms Evolved

Increased oxygen allowed for the evolution of new species that used oxygen to live. The fossil record shows that after about 1 billion years, new types of organisms evolved. These organisms were larger and more complex than prokaryotes. Called *eukaryotes,* these organisms have cells with a nucleus and other complex structures. Later, eukaryotic organisms evolved that were multicellular, or made up of more than one cell.

Mass Extinctions Occurred

Increased oxygen was followed by the evolution of some organisms, but the extinction of others. For some organisms, oxygen is toxic. Many of these organisms became extinct. Less is known about Precambrian life than life in more recent time intervals, because microscopic organisms did not preserve well in the fossil record.

12 Summarize How are cyanobacteria related to increases in oxygen in the atmosphere?

_____

_____

_____

_____

Stromatolites are cyanobacteria that form colonies and build reefs. Some of the oldest known fossils are of stromatolites. The mounds in this photo are modern stromatolites.

What defined the Paleozoic era?

The word *Paleozoic* comes from Greek words that mean "ancient life." When scientists first named this era, they thought it was the time span in which life began.

The Paleozoic era began about 542 million years ago and ended about 251 million years ago. Rocks from this era are rich in fossils of animals such as sponges, corals, snails, and trilobites. Fish, the earliest animals with backbones, appeared during this era, as did sharks.

Think Outside the Book Inquiry

13 **Compose** Select one of the organisms that lived during the Paleozoic era and find out more about it. Make a poster with information about the organism.

Life Moved onto Land

Plants, fungi, and air-breathing animals colonized land during the Paleozoic era. Land dwellers had adaptations that allowed them to survive in a drier environment. All major plant groups except flowering plants appeared. Crawling insects were among the first animals to live on land, followed by large salamander-like animals. By the end of the era, forests of giant ferns covered much of Earth, and reptiles and winged insects appeared.

A Mass Extinction Occurred

The Permian mass extinction took place at the end of the Paleozoic era. It is the largest known mass extinction. By 251 million years ago, as many as 96% of marine species had become extinct. The mass extinction wiped out entire groups of marine organisms such as trilobites. Oceans were completely changed. Many other species of animals and plants also became extinct. However, this opened up new habitats to those organisms that survived.

Visualize It!

14 **Describe** Based on this drawing, describe the landscape that existed during the Carboniferous period of the Paleozoic era.

_____

_____

_____

_____

_____

_____

Giant winged insects such as this one were common during the Carboniferous period.

This drawing is an artist's impression of life during the Carboniferous period.

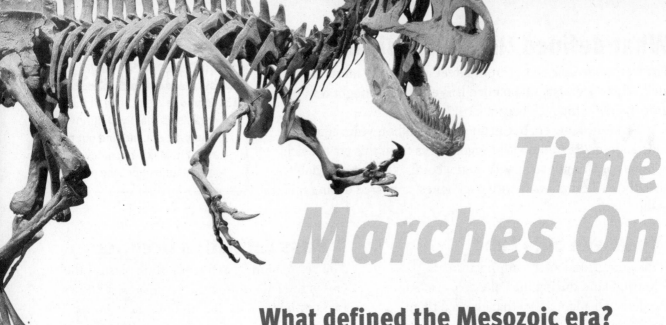

Time Marches On

What defined the Mesozoic era?

The Mesozoic era lasted about 185.5 million years. *Mesozoic* comes from Greek words that mean "middle life." Scientists think the reptiles that survived the Paleozoic era evolved into many different species during the Mesozoic era. Because of the abundance of reptiles, the Mesozoic era is commonly called the *Age of Reptiles*.

Active Reading

15 Identify As you read, underline the names of animals that lived in the Mesozoic era.

Dinosaurs and Other Reptiles Dominated Earth

Dinosaurs are the most well-known reptiles that evolved during the Mesozoic era. They dominated Earth for about 150 million years. A great variety of dinosaurs lived on Earth, and giant marine lizards swam in the ocean. The first birds and mammals also appeared. The most important plants during the early part of the Mesozoic era were conifers, or cone-bearing plants, which formed large forests. Flowering plants appeared later in the Mesozoic era.

A Mass Extinction Occurred

Why did dinosaurs and many other species become extinct at the end of the Mesozoic era? Different hypotheses are debated. Evidence shows that an asteroid hit Earth around this time. A main hypothesis is that this asteroid caused giant dust clouds and worldwide fires. With sunlight blocked by dust, many plants would have died. Without plants, plant-eating dinosaurs also would have died, along with the meat-eating dinosaurs that ate the other dinosaurs. In total, about two-thirds of all land species went extinct.

16 Summarize Make a cause-and-effect chart to explain the chain of events that, according to a main hypothesis, resulted in a mass extinction at the end of the Mesozoic era.

[chart with three boxes connected by arrows]

© Houghton Mifflin Harcourt Publishing Company • Image Credits: ©Didier Dutheil/Sygma/Corbis

What defines the Cenozoic era?

The Cenozoic era began about 65 million years ago and continues today. *Cenozoic* comes from Greek words that mean "recent life." More is known about the Cenozoic era than about previous eras, because the fossils are closer to Earth's surface and easier to find.

Primates evolved during the Cenozoic era.

Birds, Mammals, and Flowering Plants Dominate Earth

We currently live in the Cenozoic era. Mammals have dominated the Cenozoic the way reptiles dominated the Mesozoic. Early Cenozoic mammals were small, but larger mammals appeared later. Humans appeared during this era. The climate has changed many times during the Cenozoic. During ice ages, many organisms migrated toward the equator. Other organisms adapted to the cold or became extinct.

Primates Evolved

Primates are a group of mammals that includes humans, apes, and monkeys. Primates' eyes are located at the front of the skull. Most primates have five flexible digits, one of which is an opposable thumb.

The ancestors of primates were probably nocturnal, mouse-like mammals that lived in trees. The first primates did not exist until after dinosaurs died out. Millions of years later, primates that had larger brains appeared.

---

17 Hypothesize How might the mass extinction that occurred at the end of the Mesozoic era relate to the dominance of mammals in the Cenozoic era?

_____

_____

_____

_____

The Cenozoic era has been dominated by mammals. Woolly mammoths were well-adapted to surviving in a cold climate.

Visual Summary

To complete this summary, circle the correct word.
Then, use the key below to check your answers. You can
use this page to review the main concepts of the lesson.

**The fossil record provides evidence
of ancient life.**

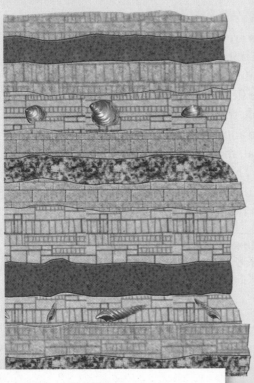

18 Absolute/Relative dating
estimates the age of a fossil
in years.

**The geologic time scale divides Earth's history
into eons, eras, periods, and epochs.**

19 Epochs/Eras are characterized by the type of
organism that dominated Earth at the time.

The **History of** **Life on Earth**

**Four major divisions of Earth's
past are Precambrian time, the
Paleozoic era, the Mesozoic era,
and the Cenozoic era.**

20 Primates evolved during the
Mesozoic era/Cenozoic era.

Answers: 18 Absolute; 19 Eras; 20 Cenozoic era

21 Synthesize Starting with Precambrian time, briefly describe how life
on Earth has changed over Earth's long history.

Lesson Review

Vocabulary

Draw a line to connect the following terms to their definitions.

1 fossil

2 geologic time scale

3 fossil record

4 extinction

A all of the fossils that have been discovered worldwide

B death of every member of a species

C trace or remains of an organism that lived long ago

D division of Earth's history into manageable parts

Key Concepts

5 List What four major divisions make up the history of life on Earth in the geologic time scale?

_____

_____

_____

_____

6 Explain What is one distinguishing feature of each of the four major divisions listed in your previous answer?

_____

_____

_____

_____

_____

_____

_____

_____

Critical Thinking

7 Contrast How do the atmospheric conditions near the beginning of Precambrian time contrast with the atmospheric conditions that are present now? Which organism is largely responsible for this change?

_____

_____

_____

Use this drawing to answer the following question.

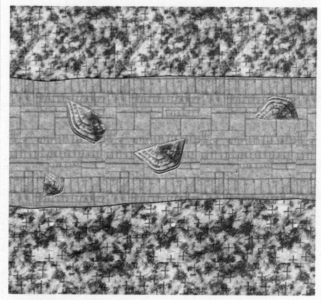

8 Explain The fossils shown are of a marine organism. In which of the three rock layers would you expect to find fossils of an organism that went extinct before the marine organism evolved? Explain your answer.

_____

_____

_____

_____

_____

My Notes

Dr. Erica Bree Rosenblum

EVOLUTIONARY BIOLOGIST

Think about watching a little frog hop around. Now, imagine a world of children who have neither seen nor heard of a frog, except in very old videos. It is true that the world's amphibian population is declining. But thanks to scientists such as Dr. Erica Bree Rosenblum, frogs will likely be part of the world for kids in future generations.

Dr. Rosenblum does research in the areas of biological diversity and adaptive evolution at the University of Idaho. Her research includes studying both the emergence of new species and the extinction of existing species. In the case of frogs, her work will hopefully prevent their extinction.

A fungus known as Bd (*Batrachochytrium dendrobatidis*) is killing many amphibians, including frogs. Since the 1980s, amphibians have declined about 70%, and this fungus is partially responsible for the decline. Dr. Rosenblum and her colleagues are studying frogs' responses to the Bd fungus under certain conditions. With continued effort, these researchers may be able to help amphibians survive this widespread fungal infection.

Frogs range in size from about one inch long to one foot long.

JOB BOARD

Vet Technician

What You'll Do: Assist veterinarians in taking care of the health of animals.

Where You Might Work: In a veterinary clinic, animal humane society, pet hospital, or zoo.

Education: A veterinarian technician license is preferred.

Other Job Requirements: You should have compassion for animals and an ability to perform a variety of tasks, including surgical assistance, laundry and exam-room cleaning, animal feeding, and dog walking.

Student Research Assistant

What You'll Do: Assist in molecular/genome research under the supervision of university faculty by recording and inputting data into the computer.

Where You Might Work: In a lab within a university building on your college campus.

Education: You must be a student within a science-based degree program at the university.

Other Job Requirements: You should be willing to work odd hours with short notice, have attention to detail, excellent data-entry skills, and an ability to follow directions carefully.

Wildlife Photographer

What You'll Do: Take photos of wildlife in their natural habitat.

Where You Might Work: For a publishing company, advertising agency, magazine, or as a freelance photographer. If you work as a freelancer, you would have to secure contracts with companies in order to be paid for your work.

Education: No degree is required; however, having an associate's or bachelor's degree in photojournalism would make it easier to get a job as a wildlife photographer. With or without a degree, you will need a portfolio of your work to take to interviews.

Classification of Living Things

ESSENTIAL QUESTION

How are organisms classified?

By the end of this lesson, you should be able to describe how people sort living things into groups based on shared characteristics.

Scientists use physical and chemical characteristics to classify organisms. Is that a spider? Look again. It's an ant mimicking a jumping spider!

Lesson Labs

Quick Labs
- Using a Dichotomous Key
- Investigate Classifying Leaves

Exploration Lab
- Developing Scientific Names

Engage Your Brain

1 Predict Check T or F to show whether you think each statement is true or false.

T	F	
☑	☐	The classification system used today has changed very little since it was introduced.
☐	☑	To be classified as an animal, an organism must have a backbone.
☑	☐	Organisms can be classified according to whether they have nuclei in their cells.
☑	☐	Scientists can study genetic material to classify organisms.
☑	☑	Organisms that have many physical similarities are always related.

2 Analyze The flowering plant shown above is called an Indian pipe. It could be mistaken for a fungus. Write down how the plant is similar to and different from other plants you know.

_____

_____

_____

_____

Active Reading

3 Word Parts Many English words have their roots in other languages. Use the Latin suffix below to make an educated guess about the meaning of the word *Plantae*.

Latin suffix	Meaning
-ae	a group of

Example sentence
Maples are part of the kingdom <u>Plantae</u>.

Plantae:

_____

_____

_____

Vocabulary Terms
- species
- genus
- domain
- Bacteria
- Archaea
- Eukarya
- Protista
- Fungi
- Plantae
- Animalia

4 Apply As you learn the definition of each vocabulary term in this lesson, write your own definition or make a sketch to help you remember the meaning of each term.

Sorting Things Out!

Why do we classify living things?

There are millions of living things on Earth. How do scientists keep all of these living things organized? Scientists *classify* living things based on characteristics that living things share. Classification helps scientists answer questions such as:

- How many kinds of living things are there?
- What characteristics define each kind of living thing?
- What are the relationships among living things?

Sharks have fins and gills.

Dolphins also have fins, but not gills.

 **Visualize It!**

5 Analyze The photos show two organisms. In the table, place a check mark in the box for each characteristic that the organisms have.

Yellow pansy butterfly

American goldfinch

	Wings	Antennae	Beak	Feathers
Yellow pansy butterfly	✓			
American goldfinch	✓			

6 Summarize What characteristics do yellow pansy butterflies have in common with American goldfinches? How do they differ?

_____

_____

_____

How do scientists know living things are related?

If two organisms look similar, are they related? To classify organisms, scientists compare physical characteristics. For example, they may look at size or bone structure. Scientists also compare the chemical characteristics of living things.

Physical Characteristics

How are chickens similar to dinosaurs? If you compare dinosaur fossils and chicken skeletons, you will see that chickens and dinosaurs share many physical characteristics. Scientists look at physical characteristics, such as skeletal structure. They also study how organisms develop from an egg to an adult. For example, animals with similar skeletons and development may be related.

Chemical Characteristics

Scientists can identify the relationships among organisms by studying genetic material such as DNA and RNA. They study mutations and genetic similarities to find relationships among organisms. Organisms that have very similar gene sequences or have the same mutations are likely related. Other chemicals, such as proteins and hormones, can also be studied to learn how organisms are related.

The two pandas below share habitats and diets. They look alike, but they have different DNA.

Red panda

The red panda is a closer relative to a raccoon than it is to a giant panda.

Raccoon

Giant panda

Spectacled bear

The giant panda is a closer relative to a spectacled bear than it is to a red panda.

7 List How does DNA lead scientists to better classify organisms?

_____

_____

_____

_____

_____

_____

What's in a Name?

How are living things named?

Early scientists used names as long as 12 words to identify living things, and they also used common names. So, classification was confusing. In the 1700s, a scientist named Carolus Linnaeus (KAR•uh•luhs lih•NEE•uhs) simplified the naming of living things. He gave each kind of living thing a two-part *scientific name*.

Scientific Names

Each species has its own scientific name. A **species** (SPEE•sheez) is a group of organisms that are very closely related. They can mate and produce fertile offspring. Consider the scientific name for a mountain lion: *Puma concolor*. The first part, *Puma*, is the genus name. A **genus** (JEE•nuhs; plural, *genera*) includes similar species. The second part, *concolor*, is the specific, or species, name. No other species is named *Puma concolor*.

A scientific name always includes the genus name followed by the specific name. The first letter of the genus name is capitalized, and the first letter of the specific name is lowercase. The entire scientific name is written either in italics or underlined.

HELLO
my name is
Carolus Linnaeus

The A.K.A. Files

Some living things have many common names. Scientific names prevent confusion when people discuss organisms.

Scientific name:
Puma concolor

Common names:
Mountain lion
Puma
Cougar
Panther

Scientific name:
Acer rubrum

Common names:
Red maple
Swamp maple
Soft maple

8 Apply In the scientific names above, circle the genus name and underline the specific name.

What are the levels of classification?

Active Reading

9 Identify As you read, underline the levels of classification.

Linnaeus's ideas became the basis for modern taxonomy (tak•SAHN•uh•mee). *Taxonomy* is the science of describing, classifying, and naming living things. At first, many scientists sorted organisms into two groups: plants and animals. But numerous organisms did not fit into either group.

Today, scientists use an eight-level system to classify living things. Each level gets more specific. Therefore, it contains fewer kinds of living things than the level above it. Living things in the lower levels are more closely related to each other than they are to organisms in the higher levels. From most general to more specific, the levels of classification are domain, kingdom, phylum (plural, *phyla*), class, order, family, genus, and species.

Classifying Organisms

Domain   **Domain Eukarya** includes all protists, fungi, plants, and animals.

Kingdom   **Kingdom Animalia** includes all animals.

Phylum   Animals in **Phylum Chordata** have a hollow nerve cord in their backs. Some have a backbone.

Class   Animals in **Class Mammalia**, or mammals, have a backbone and nurse their young.

Order   Animals in **Order Carnivora** are mammals that have special teeth for tearing meat.

Family   Animals in **Family Felidae** are cats. They are carnivores that have retractable claws.

Genus   Animals in **Genus *Felis*** are cats that cannot roar. They can only purr.

Species   The **species *Felis domesticus***, or the house cat, has unique traits that other members of genus *Felis* do not have.

From domain to species, each level of classification contains a smaller group of organisms.

Visualize It!

10 Apply What is true about the number of organisms as they are classified closer to the species level?

Triple Play

What are the three domains?

Active Reading

11 Identify As you read, underline the first mention of the three domains of life.

Once, kingdoms were the highest level of classification. Scientists used a six-kingdom system. But scientists noticed that organisms in two of the kingdoms differed greatly from organisms in the other four kingdoms. So scientists added a new classification level: domains. A **domain** represents the largest differences among organisms. The three domains are Bacteria (bak•TIR•ee•uh), Archaea (ar•KEE•uh), and Eukarya (yoo•KAIR•ee•uh).

Bacteria

All bacteria belong to Domain Bacteria. Domain **Bacteria** is made up of prokaryotes that usually have a cell wall and reproduce by cell division. *Prokaryotes* are single-cell organisms that lack a nucleus in their cells. Bacteria live in almost any environment—soil, water, and even inside the human body!

Archaea

Domain **Archaea** is also made up of prokaryotes. They differ from bacteria in their genetics and in the makeup of their cell walls. Archaea live in harsh environments, such as hot springs and thermal vents, where other organisms could not survive. Some archaea are found in the open ocean and soil.

Bacteria from the genus *Streptomyces* are commonly found in soil.

Archaea from the genus *Sulfolobus* are found in hot springs.

Eukarya

What do algae, mushrooms, trees, and humans have in common? All of these organisms are *eukaryotes*. Eukaryotes are made up of cells that have a nucleus and membrane-bound organelles. The cells of eukaryotes are more complex than the cells of prokaryotes. For this reason, the cells of eukaryotes are usually larger than the cells of prokaryotes. Some eukaryotes, such as many protists and some fungi, are single-celled. Many eukaryotes are multicellular organisms. Some protists and many fungi, plants, and animals are multicellular eukaryotes. Domain **Eukarya** is made up of all eukaryotes.

It may look like a pinecone, but the pangolin is actually an animal from Africa. It is in Domain Eukarya.

Visualize It!

12 Identify Fill in the blanks with the missing labels.

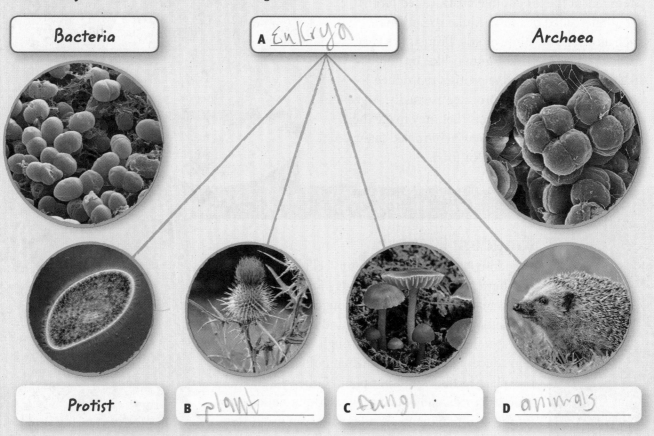

Bacteria

A Eukrya

Archaea

Protist

B plant

C fungi

D animals

13 Compare What are the differences between Bacteria and Eukarya?

_____

_____

_____

My Kingdom for a

What are the four kingdoms in Eukarya?

Scientists have classified four types of Eukarya. They ask questions to decide in which kingdom to classify an organism.

- Is the organism single-celled or multicellular?
- Does it make its food or get it from the environment?
- How does it reproduce?

Kingdom Protista

Members of the kingdom **Protista**, called *protists,* are single-celled or multicellular organisms such as algae and slime molds. Protists are very diverse, with plant-like, animal-like, or fungus-like characteristics. Some protists reproduce sexually, while others reproduce asexually. Algae are *autotrophs,* which means that they make their own food. Some protists are *heterotrophs.* They consume other organisms for food.

Kingdom Plantae

Kingdom **Plantae** consists of multicellular organisms that have cell walls, mostly made of cellulose. Most plants make their own food through the process of photosynthesis. Plants are found on land and in water that light can pass through. Some plants reproduce sexually, such as when pollen from one plant fertilizes another plant. Other plants reproduce asexually, such as when potato buds grow into new potato plants. While plants can grow, they cannot move by themselves.

14 Compare How are protists different from plants?

_____

_____

_____

Eukaryote!

Kingdom Fungi

The members of the kingdom **Fungi** get energy by absorbing materials. They have cells with cell walls but no chloroplasts. Fungi are single-celled or multicellular and include yeasts, molds, and mushrooms. Fungi use digestive juices to break down materials around them for food. Fungi reproduce sexually, asexually, or in both ways, depending on their type.

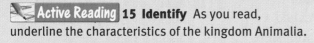 **Active Reading** **15 Identify** As you read, underline the characteristics of the kingdom Animalia.

Kingdom Animalia

Kingdom **Animalia** contains multicellular organisms that lack cell walls. They do not have chloroplasts like plants and algae, so they must get nutrients by consuming other organisms. Therefore, they are heterotrophic. Animals have specialized sense organs, and most animals are able to move around. Birds, fish, reptiles, amphibians, insects, and mammals are just a few examples of animals. Most animals reproduce sexually, but a few types of animals reproduce asexually, such as by budding.

16 Classify Place a check mark in the box for the characteristic that each kingdom displays.

Kingdom	Cells		Nutrients		Reproduction	
	Unicellular	Multicellular	Autotrophic	Heterotrophic	Sexual	Asexual
Protista	✓	✓	✓			✓
Plantae		✓	✓		✓	✓
Fungi	✓			✓	✓	✓
Animalia		✓		✓	✓	✓

How do classification systems change over time?

Millions of organisms have been identified, but millions have yet to be named. Many new organisms fit into the existing system. However, scientists often find organisms that don't fit. Not only do scientists identify new species, but sometimes these species do not fit into existing genera or phyla. In fact, many scientists argue that protists are so different from one another that they should be classified into several kingdoms instead of one. Classification continues to change as scientists learn more about living things.

How do branching diagrams show classification relationships?

How do you organize your closet? What about your books? People organize things in many different ways. Linnaeus' two-name system worked for scientists long ago, but the system does not represent what we know about living things today. Scientists use different tools to organize information about classification.

Scientists often use a type of branching diagram called a *cladogram* (KLAD•uh•gram). A cladogram shows relationships among species. Organisms are grouped according to common characteristics. Usually these characteristics are listed along a line. Branches of organisms extend from this line. Organisms on branches above each characteristic have the characteristic. Organisms on branches below lack the characteristic.

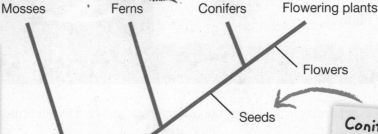

Mosses   Ferns   Conifers   Flowering plants

Flowers

Seeds

Specialized tissue for moving nutrients

Life cycle that involves spores and gametes

This branching diagram shows the relationships among the four main groups of plants.

Conifers and flowering plants are listed above this label, so they both produce seeds. Mosses and ferns, listed below the label, do not produce seeds.

© Houghton Mifflin Harcourt Publishing Company

A Class by Themselves

As scientists find more living things to study, they find that they may not have made enough classifications, or that their classifications may not describe organisms well enough. Some living things have traits that fall under more than one classification. These organisms are very difficult to classify.

Sea spider

Euglena

Euglena
An even stranger group of creatures is Euglena. Euglena make their own food as plants do. But, like animals, they have no cell walls. They have a flagellum, a tail-like structure that bacteria have. Despite having all of these characteristics, Euglena have been classified as protists.

Sea Spider
The sea spider is a difficult-to-classify animal. It is an arthropod because it has body segments and an exoskeleton. The problem is in the sea spider's mouth. They eat by sticking a straw-like structure into sponges and sea slugs and sucking out the juice. No other arthropod eats like this. Scientists must decide if they need to make a new classification or change an existing one to account for this strange mouth.

Extend

Inquiry

19 Explain In which domain would the sea spider be classified? Explain your answer.

20 Research Investigate how scientists use DNA to help classify organisms such as the sea spider.

21 Debate Find more information on Euglena and sea spiders. Hold a class debate on how scientists should classify the organisms.

Keys to Success

How can organisms be identified?

Imagine walking through the woods. You see an animal sitting on a rock. It has fur, whiskers, and a large, flat tail. How can you find out what kind of animal it is? You can use a dichotomous key.

Dichotomous Keys

A *dichotomous key* (dy•KAHT•uh•muhs KEE) uses a series of paired statements to identify organisms. Each pair of statements is numbered. When identifying an organism, read each pair of statements. Then choose the statement that best describes the organism. Either the chosen statement identifies the organism, or you will be directed to another pair of statements. By working through the key, you can eventually identify the organism.

22 Apply Use the dichotomous key below to identify the animals shown in the photographs.

Dichotomous Key to Six Mammals in the Eastern United States

1	A	The mammal has no hair on its tail.	**Go to step 2**
	B	The mammal has hair on its tail.	**Go to step 3**
2	A	The mammal has a very short naked tail.	**Eastern mole**
	B	The mammal has a long naked tail.	**Go to step 4**
3	A	The mammal has a black mask.	**Raccoon**
	B	The mammal does not have a black mask.	**Go to step 5**
4	A	The mammal has a flat, paddle-shaped tail.	**Beaver**
	B	The mammal has a round, skinny tail.	**Possum**
5	A	The mammal has a long furry tail that is black on the tip.	**Long-tailed weasel**
	B	The mammal has a long tail that has little fur.	**White-footed mouse**

A _Beaver_

B _Long-Tailed Weasle_

23 Apply Some dichotomous keys are set up as diagrams instead of tables. Work through the key below to identify the unknown plant.

© Houghton Mifflin Harcourt Publishing Company

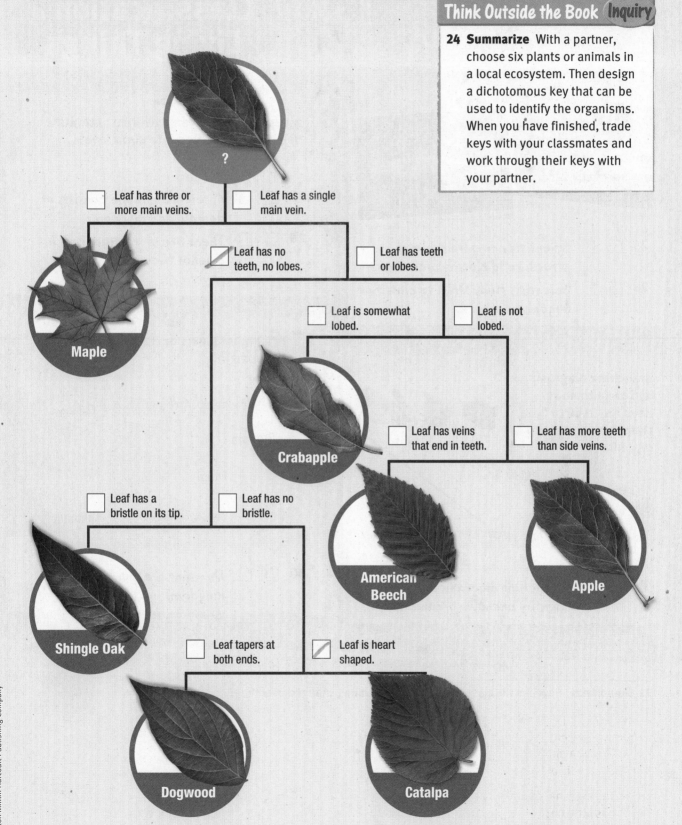

Visual Summary

To complete this summary, check the box that indicates true or false. Then, use the key below to check your answers. You can use this page to review the main concepts of the lesson.

Classification of Living Things

Scientists use physical and chemical characteristics to classify organisms.

T	F	
25 ☐	☐	Scientists compare skeletal structure to classify organisms.
26 ☐	☐	Scientists study DNA to classify organisms.

All species are given a two-part scientific name and classified into eight levels.

T	F	
27 ☐	☐	A scientific name consists of domain and kingdom.
28 ☐	☐	There are more organisms in a genus than there are in a phylum.

Branching diagrams and dichotomous keys are used to help classify and identify organisms.

T	F	
29 ☐	☐	Branching diagrams are used to identify unknown organisms.

The highest level of classification is the domain.

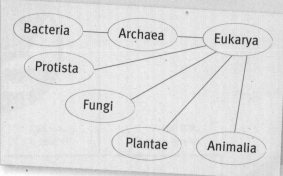

T	F	
30 ☐	☐	Domains are divided into kingdoms.

Answers: 25 T; 26 T; 27 F; 28 F; 29 F; 30 T

31 Summarize How has the classification of living things changed over time?

Unit 1 | Big Idea | The types and characteristics of organisms change over time.

Lesson 1
ESSENTIAL QUESTION
What are living things?

Describe the necessities of life and the characteristics that all living things share.

Lesson 2
ESSENTIAL QUESTION
What is the theory of evolution by natural selection?

Describe the role of genetic and environmental factors in the theory of evolution by natural selection.

Lesson 3
ESSENTIAL QUESTION
What evidence supports the theory of evolution?

Describe the evidence that supports the theory of evolution by natural selection.

Lesson 4
ESSENTIAL QUESTION
How has life on Earth changed over time?

Describe the evolution of life on Earth over time, using the geologic time scale.

Lesson 5
ESSENTIAL QUESTION
How are organisms classified?

Describe how people sort living things into groups based on shared characteristics.

Think Outside the Book

2 Synthesize Choose one of these activities to help synthesize what you have learned in this unit.

☐ Using what you learned in lessons 2, 3, and 4, explain why a scientist studying evolution might be interested in how the environment has changed over time.

☐ Using what you learned in lessons 1 and 2, write a short paragraph that compares sexual and asexual reproduction and explain why sexual reproduction is important to evolution.

Connect ESSENTIAL QUESTIONS
Lessons 2 and 3

1 Identify Describe two types of evidence that support the theory of evolution.

_____

_____

_____

_____

Vocabulary

Fill in each blank with the term that best completes the following sentences.

1 A _____ is a membrane-covered structure that contains all of the materials necessary for life.

2 In _____ reproduction, a single parent produces offspring that are genetically identical to the parent.

3 _____ is the difference in inherited traits an organism has from others of the same species.

4 The _____ is made up of fossils that have been discovered around the world.

5 In the most recent classification system, Bacteria, Archaea, and Eukarya are the three major _____ of life.

Key Concepts

Read each question below, and circle the best answer.

6 The teacher makes an argument to the class for why fire could be considered a living thing and then asks what is wrong with that argument. Tiana raises her hand and replies with one characteristic of life that fire does not have. Which of these could have been Tiana's response?

A Fire does not grow and develop.

B Fire cannot reproduce.

C Fire does not have genetic material.

D Fire does not use energy.

7 A mushroom grows on a dead, rotting oak tree lying in the forest. Which of the following best describes the tree and the mushroom?

A The oak tree was a producer, and the mushroom is a producer.

B The oak tree was a consumer, and the mushroom is a consumer.

C The oak tree was a decomposer, and the mushroom is a producer.

D The oak tree was a producer, and the mushroom is a decomposer.

8 Darwin's theory of natural selection consists of four important parts. Which of these correctly lists the four essential parts of natural selection?

  A living space, adaptation, selection, and hunting

  B overproduction, genetic variation, selection, and adaptation

  C selection, extinction, underproduction, and competition

  D asexual reproduction, genetic variation, selection, and adaptation

9 Charles Darwin studied the finches of the Galápagos Islands and found that their beaks vary in shape and size.

Darwin found that the finches that ate mostly insects had long, narrow beaks. Finches that ate mostly seeds had shorter, broad beaks to crush seeds. Which statement below best describes how natural selection resulted in the four types of finches shown above?

  A The residents of the Galápagos Islands selectively bred together finches having the traits that they wanted them to have.

  B The narrow-beaked finches came first and evolved into the broad-beaked finches through a series of natural mutations.

  C The broad-beaked finches wore down their beaks digging for insects and passed these narrower beaks on to their offspring.

  D Over time, the finches that were born with beaks better suited to the available food supply in their habitats survived and reproduced.

10 Which of these describes a likely reason why a species would become extinct after a major environmental change?

  A There are not enough members of the species born with a trait necessary to survive in the new environment.

  B The environmental changes mean fewer predators are around.

  C The change in the environment opens new resources with less competition.

  D There are more homes for the species in the changed environment.

11 Which of the following provides structural evidence for evolution?

A A fossil from the Mesozoic era shows an extinct animal similar to a modern animal.

B A comparison of similar bones in the legs of a human, a dog, and a bat.

C A genetic analysis of two animals shows similar sequences of DNA.

D The embryos of two animals look similar at similar stages.

12 The pictures below show four types of sea organisms.

1   2   3   4

Which of these would you most expect to be true if these organisms were classified by their physical characteristics only?

A Organisms 1 and 3 would be in the same species.

B Organisms 2 and 4 would be in the same genus.

C Organisms 1 and 3 would be more closely related than organisms 2 and 4.

D Organisms 2 and 4 would be more closely related than organisms 1 and 3.

13 Which of the following happened in Precambrian time?

A Life began to evolve on Earth.

B The first mammals appeared.

C A mass extinction wiped out most dinosaurs.

D Life on Earth began to move from water to land.

Critical Thinking

Answer the following questions in the space provided.

14 The dichotomous key below helps identify the order of some sharks.

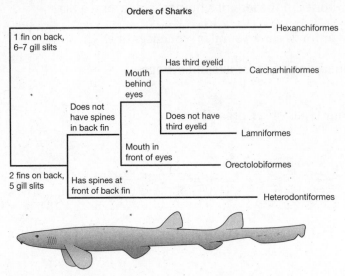

Orders of Sharks

Use the diagram to determine the order to which this shark belongs. Then name its domain and kingdom.

Order: _____

Domain: _____   Kingdom: _____

15 Describe how the changes that happened during the first division of the geologic time scale affected the evolution of organisms on Earth.

_____

_____

_____

_____

Connect **ESSENTIAL QUESTIONS**
Lessons 2, 3, 4, and 5

Answer the following question in the space provided.

16 Explain why mass extinctions occur and why they often mark divisions of geologic time.

_____

_____

_____

_____

Earth's Organisms

Big Idea

Organisms can be characterized by their structures, by the ways they grow and reproduce, and by the ways they interact with their environment.

Webbed feet allow flamingos to stand in the soft mud of their shallow water environment.

What do you think?

Organisms have many different characteristics that help them survive in their environment. Humans and birds are both animals that use two legs and two feet to move. How else are they alike? Different?

Human feet allow for walking and running easily on solid ground.

Unit 2
Earth's Organisms

Native and Nonnative Species

Some species have grown and thrived in a given area for hundreds or thousands of years. These organisms are called native species. When nonnative species are introduced, they can outcompete and outproduce the native species. The result might be a decline in or even extinction of the native species.

① Think About It

The introduction of some nonnative species has been helpful. How can initially useful organisms become harmful to an ecosystem?

_____

_____

_____

Asian carp are considered a serious threat to native fish species. Asian carp eat more of the available food and reproduce faster than the native fish populations.

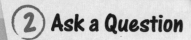

② Ask a Question

What species live in your community?

As a class, assess an area in your community to identify the native and nonnative species that live there. Check off the items on the checklist below as you consider them in your discussion.

Perch are native to the Great Lakes region. They are one species threatened by nonnative species.

Things to Consider

- ☐ What area should be assessed?

- ☐ Should garden plants and family pets be included in your assessment, or should you include only wild organisms?

- ☐ How can you determine which organisms in the assessment area are native species?

③ Make a Plan

A Describe the area that you are assessing.

_____
_____

B List the native and nonnative organisms in your assessment area.

_____
_____
_____
_____

C Choose one nonnative species and describe its impact on the assessment area. List ideas for reducing that impact in your community.

_____
_____
_____
_____
_____
_____

The Great Lakes are being threatened by nonnative species that could arrive from regional rivers or boat traffic, or through the careless release by humans of certain species directly into the lakes.

Take It Home

Do you have nonnative plants or animals in your yard or home? Discuss with an adult the pros and cons of keeping nonnative species.

Archaea, Bacteria, and Viruses

ESSENTIAL QUESTION

What are micro-organisms?

By the end of this lesson, you should be able to describe the characteristics of archaea, bacteria, and viruses, and explain how they reproduce or replicate.

Crystals of salt ring the edge of this salt lake in China. The lake is red because it is full of archaea, tiny microorganisms. The red-pigmented archaea in this lake are adapted to live in very salty environments.

© Houghton Mifflin Harcourt Publishing Company • Image Credits: (bg) ©George Steinmetz/Corbis

Lesson Labs

Quick Labs
• Observing Bacteria
• Modeling Viral Replication

Field Lab
• Culturing Bacteria from the Environment

Engage Your Brain

1 Predict Check T or F to show whether you think each statement is true or false.

T F

☐ ☐ Some bacteria are helpful.

☐ ☐ Viruses are living things.

☐ ☐ A single bacterium can produce many offspring at one time.

2 Predict Using the photo on the right and what you know of bacteria, how do you think bacteria and archaea are similar?

_____

_____

_____

_____

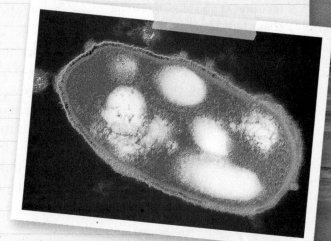

This organism is a member of the domain Archaea. It is a halophile, which means "salt lover." It lives in extremely salty environments like the one shown to the left.

Active Reading

3 Apply Many scientific words, such as *host*, also have everyday meanings. Use context clues to write your own definition for each meaning of the word *host*.

Example sentence
The <u>host</u> greeted the guests as they arrived at her house for the party.

host:

_____

_____

Example sentence
A virus takes over a <u>host</u> cell and causes it to make new viruses.

host:

_____

_____

Vocabulary Terms
• **Bacteria**   • **virus**
• **Archaea**   • **host**
• **binary fission**

4 Identify This list contains the vocabulary terms you'll learn in this lesson. As you read, circle the definition of each term.

SIZED Extra-Small

What is a prokaryote?

Active Reading

5 Identify As you read, underline characteristics of prokaryotes.

All living things fit into one of two major groups: prokaryote or eukaryote (yoo•KAIR•ee•oht). Eukaryotes are made up of one or many cells that each have a nucleus enclosed by a membrane. Prokaryotes do not have a nucleus or membrane-bound organelles and almost all are single-celled. Prokaryotes are so small we can only see them with a microscope, so they are called *microorganisms*. Prokaryotes are divided into two domains. **Bacteria** is a domain of prokaryotes that usually have a cell wall and that usually reproduce by cell division. **Archaea** (ar•KEE•uh) is a domain of prokaryotes that are genetically very different from bacteria and that have unique chemicals in their cell walls. Although they are very small, prokaryotes can get energy and reproduce, and many can move. A handful of soil may contain trillions of prokaryotes!

Visualize It!

6 On the lines below, describe the characteristics of prokaryotic cells and eukaryotic cells.

Prokaryotic Cell

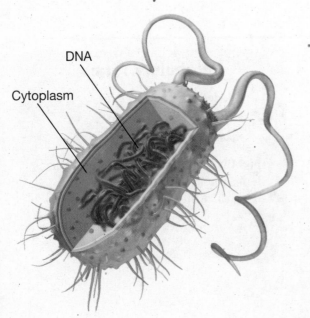

DNA

Cytoplasm

Eukaryotic Cell

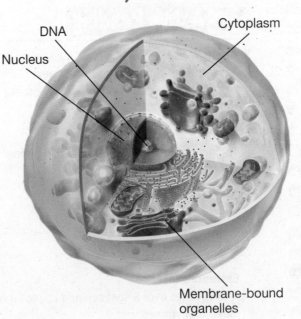

DNA

Cytoplasm

Nucleus

Membrane-bound organelles

_____

_____

What are some characteristics of archaea?

Active Reading **7 Identify** As you read, underline unusual places where archaea can live.

Archaea are organisms that have many unique molecular traits. Like bacteria, archaea are prokaryotes. But the cell walls of archaea are chemically different from those of bacteria. Some of the molecules in archaea are similar to the molecules in eukaryotes. Some of the molecules in archaea are not found in any other living things.

Archaea often live where nothing else can. Scientists have found them in the hot springs at Yellowstone National Park. They can live in extremely acidic and extremely salty habitats. They flourish near deep-sea vents where no light reaches, and they can use sulfur to convert energy. Archaea have even been found living 8 km below the Earth's surface! It was once thought that archaea only lived in extreme environments. But recent research has shown that archaea are everywhere!

8 Explain What evidence suggests that archaea are more closely related to eukaryotes than bacteria are?

_____

_____

_____

Some archaea can live in hot springs that reach near boiling temperatures.

Some archaea can live in deep-sea vents where there is no oxygen.

Beautiful Bacteria

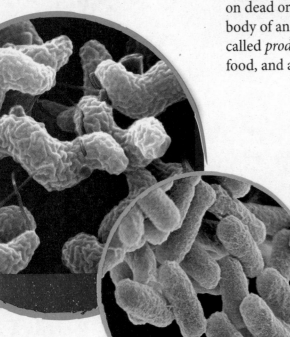

Most bacteria are round, spiral, or rod shaped.

What are some characteristics of bacteria?

Most known prokaryotes are bacteria. The domain Bacteria has more individuals than all other domains combined do. Many bacteria are *consumers* that get their nutrients by feeding on other organisms. Some bacterial consumers are *decomposers*, which feed on dead organisms. Other bacterial consumers live in or on the body of another organism. Bacteria that make their own food are called *producers*. These bacteria use energy from sunlight to make food, and are often green.

They Are Single-Celled

Bacteria are small, single-celled organisms. Some bacteria stick together to form strands or films, but usually each bacterium still functions as an independent organism. Each bacterium must take in nutrients, release energy from food, get rid of wastes, and grow on its own.

They Are Round, Spiral, or Rod Shaped

Most bacteria have a rigid cell wall that gives them their shape. Each shape helps bacteria in a different way. Bacteria that are shaped like spirals can move like corkscrews. Bacteria shaped like rods quickly absorb nutrients. Round bacteria do not dry out quickly.

 Visualize It!

9 Illustrate Draw an example of each of the three bacteria shapes described above.

© Houghton Mifflin Harcourt Publishing Company• Image Credits: (t) ©Eye of Science/Photo Researchers, Inc.; (c) ©Science Source; (b) ©Steve Gschmeissner/Science Photo Library/Getty Images

They Live Everywhere

Bacteria can be found almost everywhere on Earth. They can be found breaking down dead material in soil, making nitrogen available inside plant roots, and breaking down nutrients in animal intestines. They can be found at the tops of mountains and even in Antarctic ice. Some bacteria can survive during periods when environmental conditions become harsh by forming *endospores*. An endospore is made up of a thick, protective coating, the bacteria's genetic material, and cytoplasm. Many endospores can survive in hot, cold, and very dry places. When conditions improve, the endospores break open, and the bacteria become active again.

© Houghton Mifflin Harcourt Publishing Company • Image Credits: (bg) © Sigrid Olsson/ZenShui/Corbis; (t) © Eye of Science/Photo Researchers, Inc.; (b) ©Gary Braasch/Corbis

Active Reading

10 Relate What is the advantage for bacteria that form endospores?

_____

_____

_____

_____

A close-up look at leaves from this pond reveals that bacteria live here.

Visualize It!

11 Predict This pond is full of decaying leaves and wood as well as living aquatic plants and animals. In what parts of the pond do you think bacteria might live?

_____

_____

_____

_____

_____

_____

SPLIT Personality

In binary fission, a bacterial cell copies its DNA. The DNA separates, and the cell divides into two new cells.

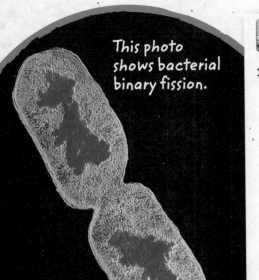

This photo shows bacterial binary fission.

How do bacteria reproduce?

Bacteria grow if they have the space and food they need. When a bacterial cell has reached its full size, it will generally begin to reproduce. Bacteria reproduce by dividing in two. Some bacteria can divide every 20 minutes!

By Binary Fission

Active Reading **12 Identify** As you read, underline the steps that occur when a bacterium reproduces using binary fission.

Both archaea and bacteria reproduce by binary fission. **Binary fission** is reproduction in which one single-celled organism splits into two single-celled organisms. The first step in bacterial reproduction is copying the cell's genetic information. Bacteria have their genetic information in the form of a long, circular strand of DNA. This loop, called a *chromosome*, is copied. Then the two chromosomes separate, with one on each side of the cell. Next, the cell's membrane starts to grow inward, separating the two halves of the cell. Finally, a new cell wall forms and separates the two new cells. At the end of binary fission, there are two identical bacterial cells, each with identical DNA. This type of reproduction, in which one parent produces offspring that are genetically identical to the parent, is called *asexual reproduction*. The cells will grow until they reach full size, and the process will begin again.

Do the Math   You Try It

13 A bacterium undergoes binary fission. After thirty minutes, both new cells are ready to divide again. If this generation divides, and so does the following generation, how many total bacteria will there be? You may want to draw a diagram to check your answer.

How do bacteria exchange DNA?

How do bacteria get new genes? There are three ways that bacteria can acquire new genetic information. One way, called *transformation,* occurs when bacteria take up DNA from the environment. Another way, *transduction,* happens when a virus injects DNA into a bacterium. Sometimes the DNA is incorporated into the cell and may be useful. The third way is called *conjugation.* Some bacteria have a second loop of DNA, smaller than the main chromosome, called a plasmid. During conjugation, a plasmid is transferred from one bacterium to another when the two bacteria temporarily join together. The bacterium that gets the plasmid now has new genes that it can use. An example of a trait found on plasmid DNA is antibiotic resistance.

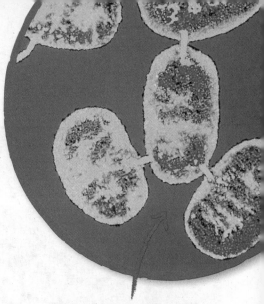

This photo shows bacterial conjugation.

 Visualize It!

14 Diagram Fill in the missing labels in this flow chart to complete the description of conjugation.

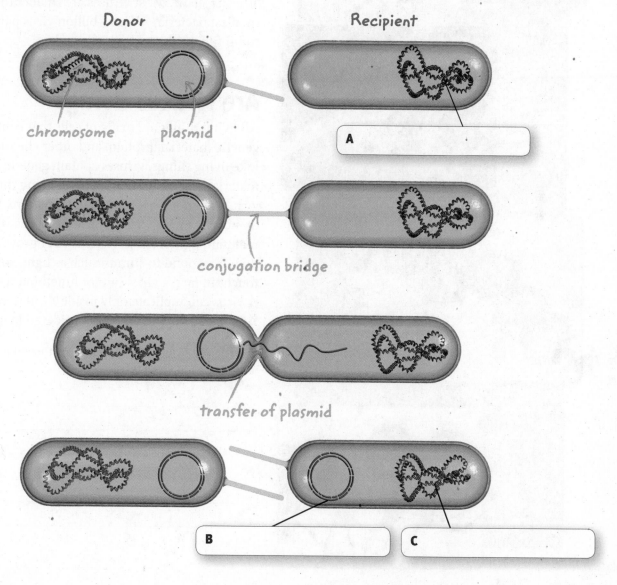

Donor   Recipient

chromosome   plasmid

A

conjugation bridge

transfer of plasmid

B   C

Alive or NOT Alive?

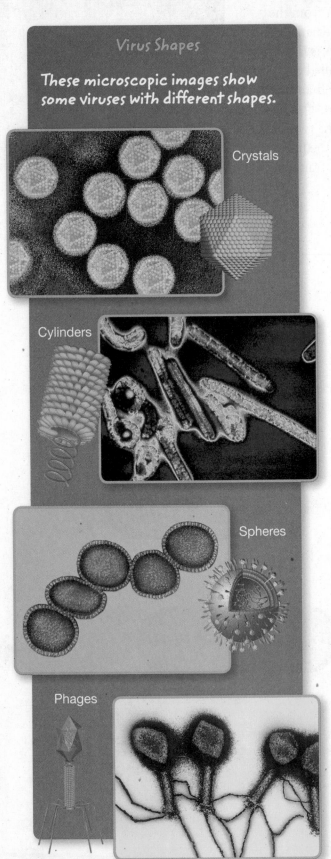

Virus Shapes

These microscopic images show some viruses with different shapes.

Crystals

Cylinders

Spheres

Phages

What are some characteristics of viruses?

A **virus** is a microscopic particle that cannot replicate on its own. It either gets inside a cell or injects a cell with its DNA, often destroying the cell. Many viruses cause diseases, such as the common cold, flu, and acquired immune deficiency syndrome (AIDS). People, plants, animals, and prokaryotes can all be infected by viruses. Viruses are made of a protein coat and genetic material. The genetic material can be either DNA or RNA. The protein coat gives the virus its shape. Most viruses are smaller than the smallest bacteria. About 5 billion virus particles could fit in a single drop of blood.

Are viruses living?

All living things are made of cells that contain genetic material, protein, and other chemicals. Like living things, viruses contain genetic material and protein. But, unlike living things, viruses do not perform any life functions. Viruses do not use energy from nutrients. Viruses do not maintain homeostasis. A virus can't grow. Viruses do not respond to stimuli such as light, sound, or touch. In fact, a virus cannot function on its own. A virus can replicate only inside a cell it infects. As a result, viruses are not considered living.

Active Reading **15 Identify** List three reasons viruses are not living things.

_____

_____

_____

_____

_____

_____

© Houghton Mifflin Harcourt Publishing Company • Image Credits: (t) ©BSIP/Photo Researchers, Inc.; (tc) ©Scott Camazine/Photo Researchers, Inc.; (b) ©Lee D. Simon/Photo Researchers, Inc.; (bc) ©Dr. Kari Lounatmaa/Science Photo Library

The Flu

You probably know someone who has had the flu. But did you know that many different influenza viruses cause the flu? Most of these viruses are not very harmful, and healthy people usually recover quickly from the flu. Sometimes, however, a new influenza virus develops that causes serious illness. A flu pandemic occurs when a new flu virus spreads to many people around the world.

The Great Pandemic

Starting in June of 1917, a particularly deadly strain of flu virus began spreading around the world. By the end of 1919, the flu had killed more than 50 million people worldwide! More than 500 million had been infected. Called the 1918 Flu, it was one of the worst epidemics in human history. Scientists are still working to understand what made this strain of flu so deadly.

Modern Threats

New strains of flu virus are constantly developing. Scientists monitor outbreaks of new strains closely. The virus that causes the outbreak is studied so that vaccines can be made.

Extend

Inquiry

16 Describe How did the 1918–1919 flu differ from other strains of the flu?

17 Research In 2009, H1N1 flu caused many cases of the flu around the world. Research how H1N1 flu differs from the 1918–1919 flu.

18 Predict How would a flu pandemic be different today than in 1918? In what ways would it be easier or harder to fight a new flu virus now?

How do viruses replicate?

Why do people stay home when they have a cold? They may not feel well enough to work or to learn. But people also want to prevent other people from getting sick. Some viruses, like the virus that causes the cold, are easily spread from person to person. How do viruses replicate and spread?

By Entering Host Cells

Because viruses are not alive, they can replicate only inside a living cell that serves as a host. A **host** is a living thing that a virus or parasite uses for resources or shelter. Viruses attack specific types of host cells. Proteins on the surface of the virus match proteins on the surface of the host cell. This allows the virus to attach to the host cell and invade it. Many viruses cannot be spread from one type of organism to another, and most can only attack certain types of cells in their host. Some viruses only attack certain types of bacteria. The tobacco mosaic virus can only attack certain types of plants, like the tomato plant shown here.

19 Explain Why can't plants catch a cold?

_____

_____

_____

_____

Both the person and the plant in these pictures are infected with viruses.

By Multiplying their DNA

The first step in viral replication occurs when a virus enters a cell or when the virus's genetic material is injected into a cell. Once the virus's genes are inside, they take over the host cell. The host cell begins following the instructions coded in the viral DNA. The host cell replicates the viral DNA. The host cell makes new protein parts for the virus. Then the parts of the new viruses assemble in the host cell. When the cell is full of new viruses, the viruses burst out of the host cell. This step, called *lysis* (LY•sis), kills the host cell. The new viruses find new host cells, and the *lytic cycle* begins again.

Some viruses insert their genes into the host cell, but new viruses are not made right away. The genes can stay inactive for a long time. When the genes do become active, they begin the lytic cycle and make copies of the virus.

Think Outside the Book Inquiry

21 Apply With a classmate, discuss why some scientists say that viruses replicate instead of reproduce.

Visualize It!

20 Identify Fill in the blank labels with the terms *virus*, *host cell*, and *new viruses* as you study the image to understand the lytic cycle.

A virus infects a host cell and injects genetic material.

A

B

Virus genetic material

The virus's genetic material takes over the host cell to make more viruses.

C

The host cell bursts, releasing new viruses.

new viruses

Visual Summary

To complete this summary, circle the correct word or words. Then use the key below to check your answers. You can use this page to review the main concepts of the lesson.

Archaea, Bacteria, and Viruses

Archaea are prokaryotes with variable cell walls made up of unique molecules.

22 Archaea are more/less similar to eukaryotes than bacteria are.

Bacteria are prokaryotes that can have a round, rod, or spiral shape.

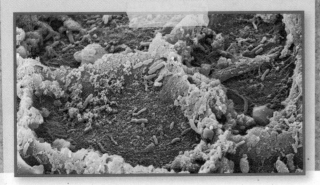

Viruses are nonliving particles made of a protein coat and genetic material.

24 Viruses are not alive because they do not release energy/have DNA or RNA.

23 Binary fission is asexual reproduction because the offspring are copies of/different from the original cell.

Answers: 22 more; 23 copies of; 24 release energy.

25 Compare What is the difference between bacterial reproduction and viral replication?

Lesson Review

Vocabulary

Fill in the blanks with the terms that best complete the following sentences.

1 A(n) _____ is made of genetic material and a protein coat.

2 _____ is when one cell reproduces by dividing in half to become two cells.

3 A virus needs a(n) _____ to reproduce.

Key Concepts

4 Compare How do prokaryotes and eukaryotes differ?

_____

_____

_____

_____

5 Describe What are the characteristics of archaea?

_____

_____

_____

_____

6 Identify In the lytic cycle, the host cell

A destroys the virus

B becomes a virus

C is destroyed

D undergoes cell division

7 Explain How do the cell walls of archaea and bacteria differ?

_____

_____

_____

_____

Critical Thinking

Use the image below to answer the question that follows.

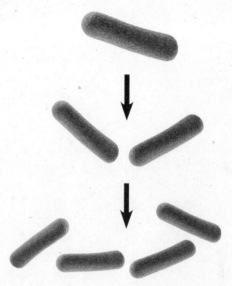

8 Explain Describe the process illustrated in the diagram above. How many individuals would exist if the process continued for one more generation?

_____

_____

_____

_____

_____

9 Apply Unlike some archaea, most bacteria die when their environment reaches extremely high temperature. How can people kill harmful bacteria that might live in some human foods?

_____

_____

_____

_____

_____

My Notes

Protists and Fungi

ESSENTIAL QUESTION

What are protists and fungi?

By the end of this lesson, you should be able to describe the characteristics of protists and fungi, and explain how they grow and reproduce.

This moth has been infected by a fungus. When the fungus sprouts, the moth dies. The fungus then bursts open, and its spores disperse.

✋ Lesson Labs

Quick Labs
- What Do Protists Look Like?
- Observing a Mushroom's Spores and Hyphae

Exploration Lab
- Survey of Reproduction in Protists and Fungi

🧠 Engage Your Brain

1 Predict Check T or F to show whether you think each statement is true or false.

T	F	
☐	☐	Mushrooms belong to the kingdom Plantae.
☐	☐	Algae use sunlight to make food through photosynthesis.
☐	☐	Spores are important in fixing atmospheric nitrogen.
☐	☐	Protists can reproduce both asexually and sexually.

2 Describe The photo below shows a protist you might be familiar with—seaweed. Write a caption for the photo that describes this protist.

_____

_____

_____

✏️ Active Reading

3 Synthesize Many English words have their roots in other languages. Use the Greek words below to make an educated guess about the meaning of the words spores and hyphae.

Latin word	Meaning
spora	seed, sowing
huphe	web

Example sentence
Fungi reproduce asexually by means of <u>spores</u>.

spores:

_____

_____

Example sentence
Mushrooms are made up of tangled <u>hyphae</u>.

hyphae:

_____

_____

Vocabulary Terms

- Protista
- gamete
- spore
- algae
- Fungi
- hyphae
- mycorrhiza
- lichen

4 Identify This list contains the vocabulary terms you'll learn in this lesson. As you read, circle the definition of each term.

On the Move!

What are some characteristics of protists?

The kingdom **Protista** is a group of eukaryotic organisms that cannot be classified as fungi, plants, or animals. Members of the kingdom Protista are called protists. Protists are a very diverse group of organisms. Many members of this kingdom are not closely related to each other and some are more closely related to members of other kingdoms. As a result, classification of protists is likely to change. So are there traits that are shared by all protists? As eukaryotes, they all have a nucleus and membrane-bound organelles.

5 Compare The two organisms shown below look very different. Why do scientists classify both as protists?

_____

_____

_____

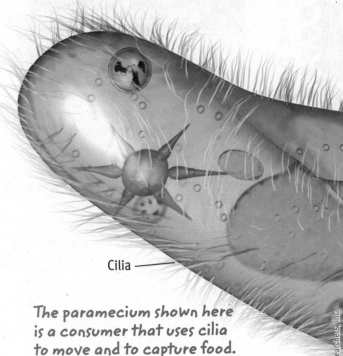

Cilia

The paramecium shown here is a consumer that uses cilia to move and to capture food.

The brown algae shown here is a multicellular protist.

They Have One or Many Cells

Most protists are single-celled organisms. These protists cannot be seen without a microscope. Diatoms are single-celled protists that have cell walls with unusual shapes. Some protists have many cells. Brown algae are multicellular protists that grow many meters long. Other protists live in colonies. Volvox, a kind of green algae, has cells that form spherical colonies. These colonies can have thousands of cells that all work together.

The diatom shown here is a microscopic single-celled protist.

They Have Membrane-Bound Organelles

Like all eukaryotes, protists have membrane-bound organelles. Organelles are structures that carry out jobs inside a cell. For example, some protists have chloroplasts that make food from the sun's energy. Many protists have contractile vacuoles that remove excess water from the cell. Some protists have organelles that sense light.

Contractile vacuole

Chloroplast

7 Identify How can structures for movement help protists to survive?

_____

_____

_____

_____

They Have Complex Structures for Movement

Some protists have structures for movement. Most protists that move do so in order to find food. Some protists use cilia to move. Cilia are hairlike structures that beat rapidly back and forth. Other protists use a flagellum or many flagella to move. A flagellum is a whiplike structure that propels the cell forward. Amoebas are protists that move by stretching their bodies. This forms a *pseudopod* (SOO•duh•pahd) or "false foot." When cytoplasm flows into the pseudopod, the rest of the cell follows.

Visualize It!

6 Draw Each protist shown below is missing the structures it uses for movement. Draw the missing parts for each individual.

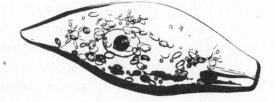

Flagellum

The euglena is a producer that uses light to make food. It uses its flagellum to move toward light and to escape from predators.

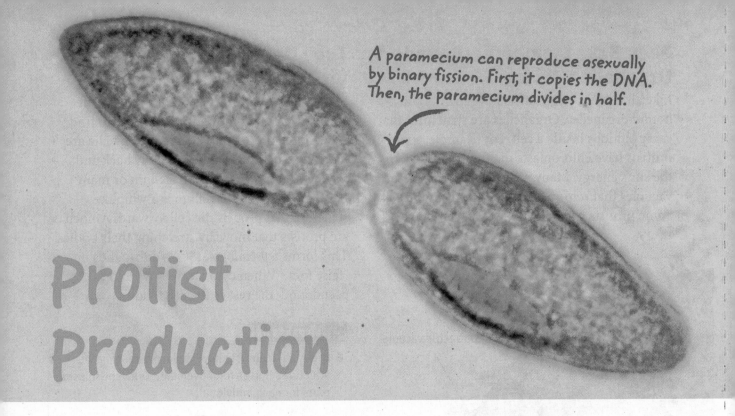

A paramecium can reproduce asexually by binary fission. First, it copies the DNA. Then, the paramecium divides in half.

Protist Production

How can protists reproduce?

Some protists reproduce only asexually. Others reproduce asexually at one stage in their life cycle and sexually at another stage. For some protists, the type of reproduction alternates by generation. For example, a parent reproduces asexually, and its offspring reproduce sexually. Then the cycle starts again. Other protists reproduce asexually until environmental conditions become stressful. A lack of food or water can trigger these protists to reproduce sexually until conditions improve.

By Asexual Reproduction

Most protists can reproduce asexually. In asexual reproduction, the offspring come from just one parent. So every organism can produce offspring on its own. These offspring are genetically identical to the parent. When environmental conditions are favorable and there is plenty of food and water, asexual reproduction produces many offspring very quickly.

Protists can reproduce asexually in different ways. These include binary fission and fragmentation. During binary fission, a single-celled protist copies its DNA. The protist then divides into two cells. Each new cell has a copy of the DNA. The paramecium shown above is splitting through binary fission. Fragmentation is a process in which a piece breaks off of an organism and develops into a new individual. Many multicellular protists can reproduce by fragmentation.

Active Reading

8 Identify On this page and the next, underline the benefits of asexual reproduction and the benefits of sexual reproduction.

Think Outside the Book

9 Compare Both protists and bacteria can reproduce asexually using binary fission. Research to find out how protist fission differs from bacterial fission.

© Houghton Mifflin Harcourt Publishing Company • Image Credits: ©Lester V. Bergman/Corbis

By Sexual Reproduction

Some protists reproduce sexually. In sexual reproduction, two cells, called **gametes**, join together. Each gamete contains a single copy of the genes for the organism. A cell with only one copy of genetic material is described as being *haploid.* A cell with two copies is *diploid.* Each gamete comes from a different parent. When the haploid gametes join, the diploid offspring have a unique combination of genetic material. Genetic diversity increases a species' chance of survival when the environment changes.

In some protists, generations alternate between using sexual or asexual reproduction. The haploid generation adults are called *gametophytes* (guh•MEET•uh•fyts). The diploid generation adults are called *sporophytes* (SPOHR•uh•fyts). Diploid adults undergo meiosis to make haploid spores. **Spores** are reproductive cells that are resistant to stressful environmental conditions. These spores develop into haploid adults. The haploid adults undergo mitosis to form haploid gametes. Two gametes join to form a diploid zygote. The zygote then grows into a diploid adult. This continuing cycle is called *alternation of generations.*

Ulva, or sea lettuce, is an algae that reproduces by alternation of generations.

👁 Visualize It!

10 Draw Use the terms *diploid*, *haploid*, and *adult* to fill in the blanks describing how *Ulva* reproduces with alternating generations of diploid and haploid cells.

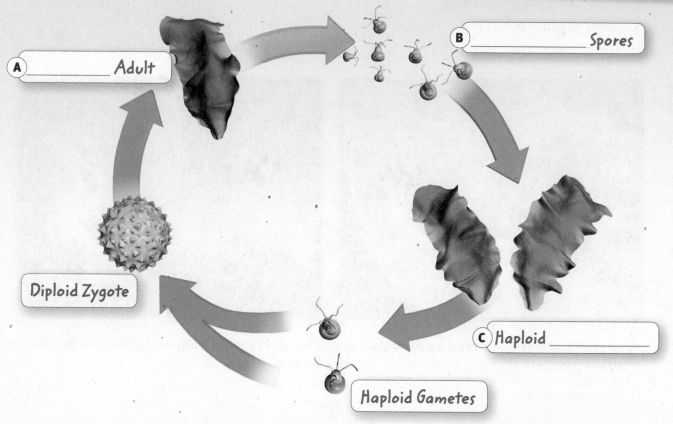

A _____ Adult

B _____ Spores

Diploid Zygote

C Haploid _____

Haploid Gametes

A Diverse Group

What are different kinds of protists?

Because protists are so diverse, grouping them can be difficult. One useful way to group protists is by how they get food. Some capture food, like animals do. Some absorb nutrients, like fungi do. Some make food, like plants do.

> **Active Reading** **11 Identify** On this page and the next, underline how each kind of protist gets its food.

Animal-like Protists

Animal-like protists cannot make their own food. Instead, they get nutrients by ingesting other organisms. Many animal-like protists eat small organisms such as bacteria, yeast, or other protists.

Most animal-like protists can move around their environment. This allows them to search for food in the environment. Sometimes, the same structures that aid movement can also help protists get food. For example, cilia sweep food toward a paramecium's food passageway. Amoebas use their pseudopodia to engulf their food.

Fungus-like Protists

Usually, fungus-like protists cannot move on their own. So capturing live organisms would be hard for these protists. Since they cannot make their own food, how do they get nutrients? Fungus-like protists absorb nutrients from the environment. Many fungus-like protists absorb nutrients from living or dead organisms.

Fungus-like protists produce spores that are used in reproduction. The protists release the spores into the environment, and the spores can survive through periods of harsh conditions. When the spores land on a good source of nutrients, they develop into an adult.

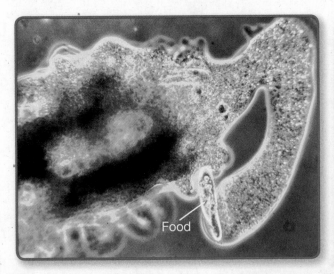

Amoebas capture their food by surrounding it with a pseudopod.

Food

This water mold absorbs nutrients from the body of a fish.

Plant-like Protists

Plant-like protists are producers. This means they use the sun's energy to make food through photosynthesis. Single-celled, free-floating, plant-like protists are a main part of the ocean's phytoplankton. Phytoplankton are tiny, floating organisms that provide food for many larger organisms. They also produce much of the world's oxygen.

Multicellular plant-like protists are called **algae**. All algae have the green pigment chlorophyll in their cells. Many also have other pigments. Algae are grouped by color. The three main groups of algae are brown algae, red algae, and green algae. The pigment color determines what wavelengths of light the algae can absorb.

12 Infer Because plant-like protists make their own food from sunlight, in what kind of environment would they not be able to survive? Why?

_____
_____
_____
_____
_____
_____

Red algae live in tropical water.

Some brown algae can grow to be many meters long.

This green algae lives in shallow tide pools.

13 Summarize For each kind of protist on the chart below, list three characteristics:

Animal-like Protists	Fungus-like Protists	Plant-like Protists

Lots of Fun(gi)!

What are some characteristics of fungi?

Fungi (FUHN•jy; singular, fungus) are spore-producing organisms that absorb nutrients from the environment. Fungi are so different from other organisms that they are placed in their own kingdom.

Fungi are *consumers*, which means they cannot make their own food. Also, fungi cannot move. This means they cannot catch organisms to ingest as food. Fungi get nutrients by secreting digestive juices onto a food source. Then, they absorb nutrients from the dissolved food. Many fungi are *decomposers*. Decomposers get nutrients from dead matter.

All fungi are made of eukaryotic cells that have nuclei. Fungi are unique because their cell walls contain *chitin*. Chitin is a hard substance that strengthens the cell walls. Some fungi are single-celled. Most are made up of many cells that form chains. These chains are threadlike fungal filaments called **hyphae** (HY•fee; singular, hypha).

We can only see a small part of many fungi. That's because most of the organism is underground or woven into its food source. Most hyphae in a fungus form a twisted mass called a *mycelium* (mie•SEE•lee•uhm). The hidden mycelium makes up the major part of the body of a fungus. Just a small part of a fungus is visible. The visible part of a mushroom includes a stalk, a cap, and gills that release spores.

Cap

Gills

Stalk

Mycelium

Thread-like strands called hyphae make up the body of this mushroom. Most of the hyphae are underground.

Hyphae

How can fungi reproduce?

Fungi reproduce both asexually and sexually. In asexual reproduction, offspring are genetically identical to the parent. In sexual reproduction, offspring are genetically unique.

By Asexual Reproduction

Asexual reproduction in fungi occurs in three ways. In fragmentation, hyphae break apart, and each piece becomes a new fungus. In budding, a small portion of a parent cell pinches off to become a new individual. In asexual reproduction by spores, hyphae produce a long stalk called a *sporangium* (spuh•RAN•jee•uhm). Here, spores develop through mitosis. Spores are light and easily spread by wind. So spores can travel long distances even though fungi cannot move on their own. When conditions are favorable, a spore develops into a new fungus.

By Sexual Reproduction

In most fungi, sexual reproduction occurs when hyphae from two individuals join together. The fused hyphae produce a special reproductive structure, such as a mushroom. Genetic material from both individuals fuse to form diploid cells. Then the cells undergo meiosis to become haploid again. The spores are then released. These spores are much like asexual spores. Both can spread easily through the environment and survive until favorable conditions arise.

Active Reading **15 Identify** Describe the role of spores in both asexual and sexual fungus reproduction.

_____

_____

This bread mold sporangium will release spores to spread through the environment.

This collared earthstar fungus releases its spores by shooting them into the air.

Inquiry

16 Infer Why is it important for spores to spread easily to other locations?

_____

_____

What are some kinds of fungi?

Fungi are classified based on their shape and the way they reproduce. Many species of fungi fit into three main groups. These groups are zygote fungi, sac fungi, and club fungi.

 **Active Reading** **17 Identify** On this page and the next, underline the characteristics that define each kind of fungus.

Zygote Fungi

Zygote fungi are named for sexual reproductive structures that produce zygotes inside a tough capsule. Most of the fungi in this group live in the soil and are decomposers. Some zygote fungi are used to process foods like soybeans. Other types of zygote fungi are used to fight bacterial infections. However, some zygote fungi can cause problems for people. Have you ever seen moldy bread? A mold is a fast-growing, fuzzy fungus that reproduces asexually. Bread mold and molds that rot fruits and vegetables are examples of this asexual stage of a zygote fungus life cycle. Some molds also have a stage during which they reproduce sexually.

This bread mold is a fuzzy example of a zygote fungus.

Morels are an edible type of sac fungus that grow at the base of trees.

Sac Fungi

Sac fungi are the largest group of fungi. Sac fungi include yeasts, powdery mildews, morels, and bird's-nest fungi. Sac fungi reproduce asexually and sexually. Sexually produced spores develop within a microscopic sac that then opens to release the spores. This structure gives sac fungi their name. Most sac fungi are multicellular. Yeasts are typically single-celled sac fungi that usually reproduce asexually by budding. Budding occurs when a new cell pinches off from an existing cell. Under certain conditions a yeast will reproduce sexually and form spores in sacs. Yeasts are used to make bread and alcohol. Other sac fungi make antibiotics and vitamins.

These mushrooms are club fungi.

Club Fungi

Mushrooms, bracket fungi, puffballs, smuts, and rusts are club fungi. Club fungi are named for the microscopic structures in which the spores develop. Only the spore-producing part of a club fungus is visible. These structures usually grow at the edges of the mycelium. A fungal mycelium can be incredibly large. One of the world's largest living organisms is a honey mushroom in Oregon whose mycelium spans almost 9 km^2.

Club fungi are very important decomposers of wood. Without fungi, the nutrients in wood could not be recycled. Smuts and rusts are plant parasites. They often attack crops such as corn and wheat.

These red **Amanita** are highly toxic, yet beautiful, club fungi.

How do fungi form partnerships?

Fungi form two very important partnerships. Some fungi grow on or in the roots of plants. These plants provide nutrients to the fungus. In return, the fungus usually helps the roots absorb minerals. This partnership is called a **mycorrhiza** (my•kuh•RY•zuh).

A **lichen** is a partnership between a fungus and a green alga or cyanobacterium. They are so inseparable that scientists give lichens their own scientific names. The alga or cyanobacterium uses photosynthesis to make food. The fungus gives protection, water, and minerals. Lichens provide food for animals in polar climates. Also, because lichens are very sensitive to pollution, the presence of lichens indicates that an environment has clean air.

18 Infer Suppose that the number of kinds of lichens at a city park is decreasing each year. What might explain this disappearance?

_____

_____

_____

Lichens can grow on rocks. They release acids that break down rock over time to make soil.

Visual Summary

To complete this summary, fill in the blank with the correct word or phrase. Then use the key below to check your answers. You can use this page to review the main concepts of the lesson.

Protists are eukaryotes that don't fit in other classification groups.

19 A _____ is a haploid reproductive cell used in sexual reproduction.

Protists and Fungi

Protists can be grouped as fungus-like, plant-like, and animal-like protists.

20 _____-like protists can produce their own food from the sun's energy.

Fungi absorb nutrients and have chitinous cell walls.

21 Fungi are _____ because they have a nucleus and other membrane-bound organelles.

Fungi can partner with other organisms.

22 _____ can indicate levels of air pollution.

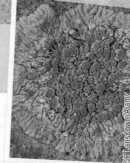

Answers: 19 gamete; 20 plant; 21 eukaryotes; 22 lichens

23 Describe This lesson groups protists informally by the way they get food. Think of another way to categorize the different kinds of protists and describe your system below.

Lesson Review

Vocabulary

Draw a line to connect the following terms to their definitions.

1 fungi

2 protists

3 spore

4 gamete

A reproductive cell that resists harsh environmental conditions

B extremely diverse group of eukaryotic organisms; some have cilia

C reproductive cell that unites with another reproductive cell

D spore-producing organisms that absorb nutrients

Key Concepts

5 Compare Why are protists discussed in groups such as animal-like, plant-like, and fungus-like protists?

_____

_____

_____

_____

6 List Write the three major types of fungi and an example of each.

_____

_____

_____

_____

7 Identify What are two ways that protists can reproduce asexually?

_____

_____

8 Describe What are two ways in which fungi reproduce?

_____

_____

_____

Critical Thinking

Use this image to answer the following question.

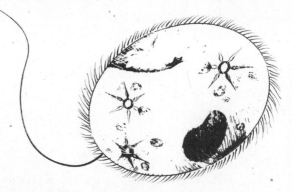

9 Hypothesize Do you think this protist can make its own food? Explain.

_____

_____

_____

_____

10 Synthesize In humans, infections by fungi and protists are usually more difficult to treat than bacterial infections. Suggest an explanation that is based on cell structure.

_____

_____

_____

_____

11 Apply Suppose that when crops developed a fungal infection, a farmer decided to spray the soil with a fungicide. Just after spraying, the plants looked healthier, but soon they showed signs of mineral deficiency. What might explain this response?

_____

_____

_____

_____

My Notes

Introduction to Plants

ESSENTIAL QUESTION

What are plants?

By the end of this lesson, you should be able to list the characteristics that all plants share, and explain how plants are classified into major plant divisions.

Is this an alien spacecraft? No, it's a passion flower plant! Plants come in many different shapes and sizes.

 Engage Your Brain

1 Predict Check T or F to show whether you think each statement is true or false.

T	F	
☐	☐	All plants have a special transport system that delivers water and nutrients.
☐	☐	The majority of plants have roots, stems, and leaves.
☐	☐	Conifer trees, such as pine trees, produce flowers.
☐	☐	Plants are multicellular eukaryotes.

2 Categorize Write a caption for this magnified cross section of a buttercup plant stem.

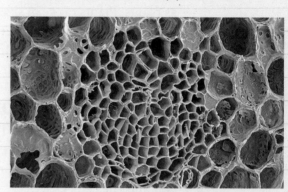

_____

_____

_____

Active Reading

3 Synthesize You can often define an unknown word if you know the meaning of its word parts. Use the word parts and sentences below to make an educated guess about the meaning of the words *gymnosperm* and *angiosperm*.

Word part	Meaning
gymno-	naked, bare
angio-	vessel, container
sperm	seed

Example sentence
Gymnosperms are seed plants that do not produce fruit.

gymnosperm:

_____

Example sentence
Angiosperms are seed plants that do produce fruit.

angiosperm:

_____

Vocabulary Terms

- producers
- photosynthesis
- chlorophyll
- vascular system
- seed
- pollen
- gymnosperm
- angiosperm

4 Identify As you learn the definition of each vocabulary term in this lesson, create your own definition or sketch to help you remember the meaning of the term.

Plants Alive

What are the characteristics of plants?

The kingdom Plantae includes a wide variety of organisms known as plants. Plants range in size from the tallest giant sequoia trees, reaching more than 80 meters (270 ft) to the smallest flowering plant, which can fit on the tip of your finger. So what do these plants have in common with one another?

They Are Multicellular Eukaryotes

All plants are multicellular. Their bodies are made up of more than one cell. They are also eukaryotes. This means that their cells contain membrane-bound organelles, including a nucleus which contains the cell's DNA.

They Have a Two-Stage Life Cycle

All plants have a life cycle that is made up of two stages: a *sporophyte* stage and a *gametophyte* stage. These are the two stages in which plants reproduce and disperse to new areas. In the sporophyte stage, plants make spores that are genetically identical to the parent plant. In a suitable environment, such as in damp soil, spores can grow into new plants that are the gametophytes.

In the gametophyte stage, plants produces gametes. Female gametophytes produce eggs. Male gametophytes produce sperm. Eggs and sperm are sex cells. By themselves, the sex cells cannot grow directly into new plants. For a new plant to be produced, a sperm cell must fuse with, or *fertilize*, an egg. This type of reproduction is called sexual reproduction. The fertilized egg can grow into a sporophyte, and the cycle can begin again.

Chlorophyll gives plants their green color.

Think Outside the Book

5 Apply Imagine a plant is running for president of the garden club. Write a campaign speech stating its unique characteristics.

© Houghton Mifflin Harcourt Publishing Company • Image Credits: ©HMH

They Have Walls and Vacuoles

Plant cells are surrounded by a rigid cell wall that lies outside the cell membrane. The cell wall supports and protects the plant cell. The cell wall also determines the size and shape of a plant cell. A chemical called *cellulose* is the main component of plant cell walls. The strength of the cell wall helps plants stand upright. Some plant cells also have a *secondary cell wall*. This wall forms after the cell is mature, and gives woody plants their strength. Once the secondary cell wall forms, the plant cell cannot grow larger.

Inside a plant cell is a large central vacuole. The vacuole is a membrane-bound organelle that stores water and also helps to keep the plant upright. When the vacuole is full, water presses on the inside of the cell wall. This keeps the cell firm, like an inflated balloon. If the vacuole loses water, the pressure inside the cell decreases, and the plant begins to wilt.

They Make Their Own Food

Almost all plants are producers. **Producers** make their own food by using energy from their surroundings. The process by which plants and other organisms convert solar energy to chemical energy is called **photosynthesis** (foh•toh•SIN•thih•sis).

In plants, photosynthesis occurs in an organelle called a chloroplast. Chloroplasts contain special pigments called chlorophyll. **Chlorophyll** (KLOHR•uh•fil) is a green pigment that captures energy from sunlight. Chloroplasts use this energy, along with carbon dioxide and water, to make food in the form of a sugar called *glucose*. It is chlorophyll that gives plants their green color.

Active Reading **6 Identify** Name the function of chlorophyll in plants.

 **Visualize It!**

7 Identify In which part of the cell is chlorophyll found?

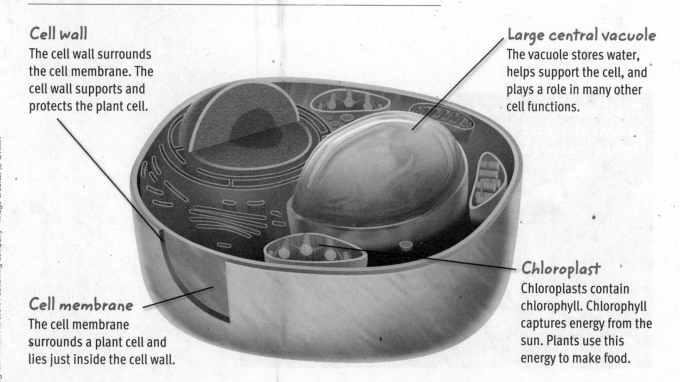

Cell wall
The cell wall surrounds the cell membrane. The cell wall supports and protects the plant cell.

Large central vacuole
The vacuole stores water, helps support the cell, and plays a role in many other cell functions.

Cell membrane
The cell membrane surrounds a plant cell and lies just inside the cell wall.

Chloroplast
Chloroplasts contain chlorophyll. Chlorophyll captures energy from the sun. Plants use this energy to make food.

A Wide World of Plants

What are the two main groups of plants?

Plants can be grouped into two broad categories: nonvascular plants and vascular plants. A plant that has a vascular system is called a vascular plant. A **vascular system** is a system of tube-like tissues that transports water, nutrients, and other materials from one part of an organism to another part. Nonvascular plants do not have a vascular system.

Nonvascular Plants

Have you ever walked through a cool forest with a moist green carpet on the ground? Chances are, the green "carpet" was made up of tiny plants called moss. Mosses, and their relatives such as liverworts and hornworts, are nonvascular plants. Nonvascular plants do not have vascular systems to transport water and nutrients throughout their bodies. Instead, water must move from the environment and throughout the plant by a process called *diffusion*. If nonvascular plants were large, the cells of the plants that are far from the ground would not get enough water. Likewise, cells that are far from the leaves would not get enough nutrients. For this reason, nonvascular plants are all fairly small.

Active Reading **8 Explain** Why are nonvascular plants so small?

This giant sequoia transports water and nutrients through a vascular system. The materials move between the roots and the leaves, nearly 72 m (200 ft) above ground.

This liverwort is a type of nonvascular plant. The liverwort stalks are about 1 cm tall.

Vascular Plants

Vascular plants have a vascular system that transports water and nutrients throughout the plant's body. The vascular system allows these plants to grow large and still move water and materials effectively. As a result, many vascular plants are very tall. Some, such as the giant redwoods of California, reach heights of over 91 meters (300 ft)!

The body of a vascular plant is divided into two systems: the root system and the shoot system. The root system is made up of roots and other underground structures. The above ground structures, such as stems, leaves and flowers, make up the shoot system. Roots, stems, and leaves are the three major kinds of organs in vascular plants. Water and materials are transported between the roots and the shoots through vascular tissue.

Active Reading

9 List As you read, underline the importance of a plant's vascular system.

Leaves

Most leaves grow above ground. They make food for the plant by photosynthesis. The outer surfaces of a leaf are covered by a waxy cuticle that prevents water loss. Tiny openings in leaves, called *stomata,* allow for gas exchange.

Stem

Stems are usually above ground. They provide support, and they transport water and minerals from the roots up to the leaves. Stems also transport the glucose that is made in the leaves to other parts of the plant. Some stems store materials, such as water.

Roots

Most roots are underground. They supply plants with water and minerals from the soil. Roots also anchor plants in the soil and can store extra food made through photosynthesis.

10 Compare In the table below, compare the functions of the three parts of the plant.

Roots	Stems	Leaves

Spore Power to Ya!

How are seedless nonvascular plants classified?

When you think of growing a plant, you probably imagine planting a seed. But not all plants make seeds. In fact, all nonvascular plants and some vascular plants are seedless. These plants, like all plants, spread by producing spores.

Mosses

Mosses grow on moist soil or on rocks, forming a fuzzy mat of tiny green plants. Mosses have leafy stalks and rhizoids (RY•zoydz). A *rhizoid* is a nonvascular rootlike structure that helps mosses attach to surfaces such as rocks and trees. Rhizoids help the plants get water and nutrients. Mosses can grow even in harsh environments. They have been found above the tree line on mountains and can survive even the freezing temperatures of Antarctica!

Liverworts and Hornworts

Like mosses, liverworts and hornworts are small nonvascular plants that usually live in damp environments. Liverworts can be leafy and mosslike or broad and flattened. Hornworts also have broad, flattened leaflike structures. Both liverworts and hornworts have rhizoids to hold them in place.

11 Identify As you read, underline the structure in nonvascular plants that is like a root.

Mosses and other nonvascular seedless plants dominated the land for many millions of years.

Visualize It!

12 Inquiry Study the photo of the moss. What evidence suggests that mosses produce their own food?

_____

_____

_____

© Houghton Mifflin Harcourt Publishing Company • Image Credits: ©Birgit Koch/Age Fotostock/America, Inc.

How are seedless vascular plants classified?

Seedless vascular plants include ferns, horsetails, and club mosses. These plants all have vascular tissue, and generally have roots, stems, and leaves. Like seedless nonvascular plants, seedless vascular plants reproduce using spores.

Ferns and Whisk Ferns

Ferns are seedless vascular plants often grown as house plants. Ferns have roots, and most ferns also have rhizomes that help them spread. A *rhizome* (RY•zohm) is an underground stem from which new leaves and roots grow. Ferns have leaves, called *fronds*, that uncurl as they grow. Whisk ferns are related to ferns, but look very different. They have rhizoids instead of roots, and small growths that look like buttons instead of leaves.

Horsetails

Horsetails have cane-like stems with leaves that grow in a unique whorl pattern around the stems. Horsetails can be up to eight meters tall, but many are smaller. They usually grow in wet, marshy places. Their stems are hollow and contain silica. The silica gives horsetails a gritty, rough texture. In fact, early American pioneers used horsetails to scrub pots and pans.

Club Mosses

Club mosses look similar to true mosses. But unlike true mosses, club mosses have vascular tissue, roots, stems, and tiny leaves. Prehistoric club mosses were tall trees. Some even grew up to 40 m tall! Today's club mosses are small. An example of a modern club moss is the ground pine. Like the name suggests, the ground pine looks like a miniature pine tree. Club mosses grow in woodlands and near streams and marshes.

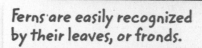
Ferns are easily recognized by their leaves, or fronds.

On the underside of a fern frond are clusters of spore-producing containers called sori.

13 Compare In the graphic organizer below, compare seedless nonvascular plants to seedless vascular plants. How are they similar and different?

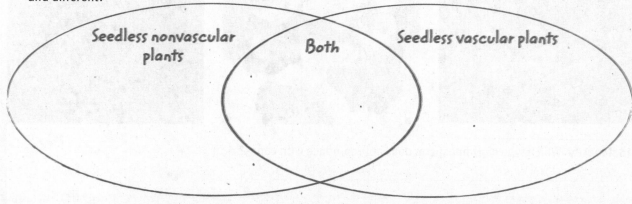

Seedless nonvascular plants   Both   Seedless vascular plants

Seeds of Success

How are seed plants classified?

Seed plants are vascular plants that reproduce by making seeds. A **seed** is a plant embryo enclosed in a protective coating. Seed plants also produce **pollen**, a tiny structure in which sperm forms. A sperm cell from pollen fertilizes an egg cell, which develops into an embryo inside a seed. Seed plants are classified based on whether or not their seeds are enclosed in a fruit.

Gymnosperms

Gymnosperms (JIM•nuh•spermz) are plants that produce seeds that are not enclosed in a fruit. This group includes cycads (SY•kadz), ginkgoes (GING•kohz), and conifers. Cycads produce seeds in large, woody structures called *cones* that grow at the center of a thick trunk. Ginkgoes produce round, grape-like seeds that are not covered by a cone. Ginkgo seeds smell like rotting butter. The word *conifer* comes from two words that mean "cone-bearing." Conifers, such as pine trees, also produce cones. The wood of conifer trees is used for building and for paper products. Pine trees also produce a sticky fluid called resin used to make soap, paint, and ink.

Active Reading

14 Identify As you read, underline the characteristics of gymnosperms.

Cycads are gymnosperms found in the tropics that have short stems and palm-like leaves. Cycads produce seeds on large, protective cones. Only about 140 species of cycads still exist.

Ginkgoes are gymnosperms that are pollution tolerant and are used in traditional medicine. Only the *Ginkgo biloba* is still alive today. Its leaves are fan-shaped, and its seeds are round and not covered by a cone.

Conifers are the most common type of gymnosperm. This group includes pine trees, cedars, redwoods, and junipers. They produce seeds in cones and have needle-like leaves. Many are green all year.

15 Identify Which type of gymnosperm does not reproduce with cones?

_____

Angiosperms

Angiosperms (AN•jee•uh•spermz) are vascular plants that produce flowers, and fruits which surround and protect seeds. Angiosperms are the most abundant type of plant alive today. At least 260,000 living species of angiosperms are known, and new species are still being discovered. They can be found in almost every ecosystem.

Flowers are the reproductive structures of angiosperms. Flowers are typically made up of sepals, petals, stamens, and a pistil. Sepals are modified leaves that cover and protect the flower while it is budding. Flower petals are often colorful and fragrant. A stamen is the male reproductive structure in a flower. It is made up of an anther, which is attached to a filament. Pollen is made in the anther. A pistil is the female reproductive structure in a flower. The seed develops within the ovary at the base of the pistil. As the seed develops, the ovary matures into a fruit which covers the seed.

 **Visualize It!**

16 Label Fill in the structure of each of the flower parts described below.

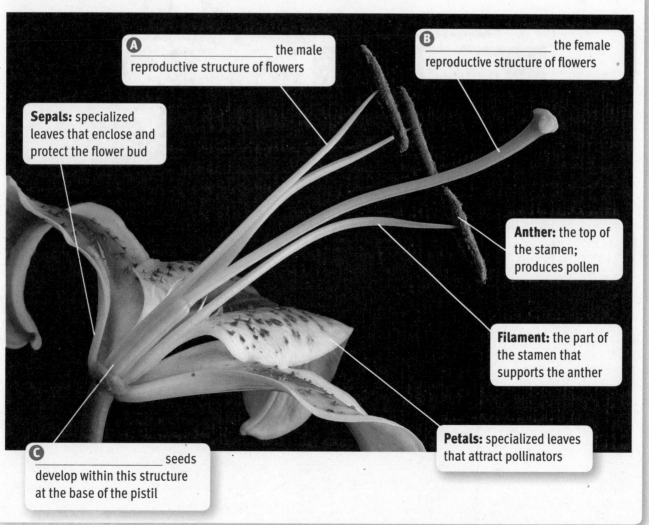

A _____ the male reproductive structure of flowers

B _____ the female reproductive structure of flowers

Sepals: specialized leaves that enclose and protect the flower bud

Anther: the top of the stamen; produces pollen

Filament: the part of the stamen that supports the anther

Petals: specialized leaves that attract pollinators

C _____ seeds develop within this structure at the base of the pistil

Visualize It!

17 Compare Compare vascular and nonvascular plants, seedless and seed vascular plants, and nonflowering and flowering plants.

Nonvascular plants

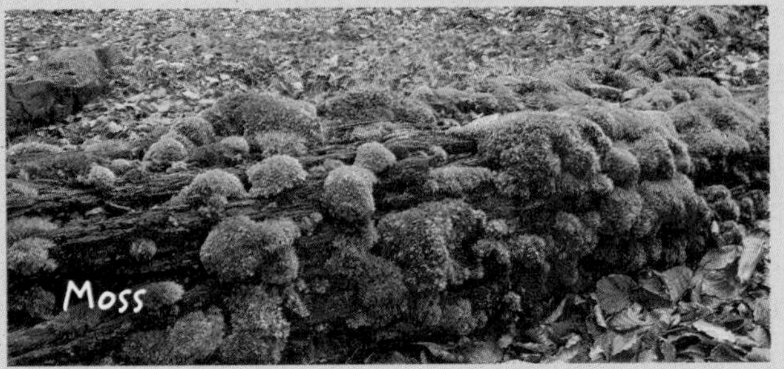
Moss

Vascular plants

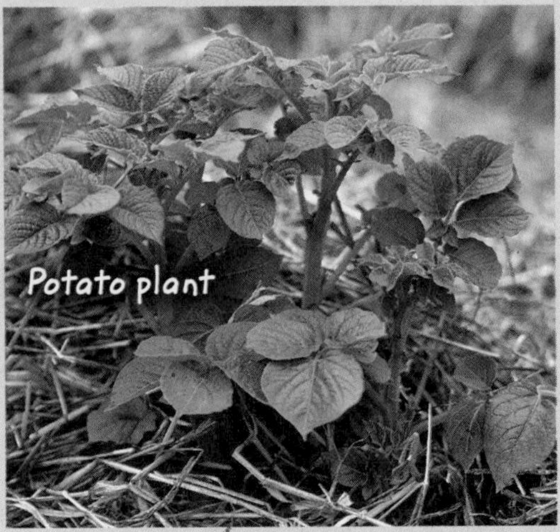
Potato plant

A Summarize the similarities and differences.

____

____

____

Seedless vascular plants

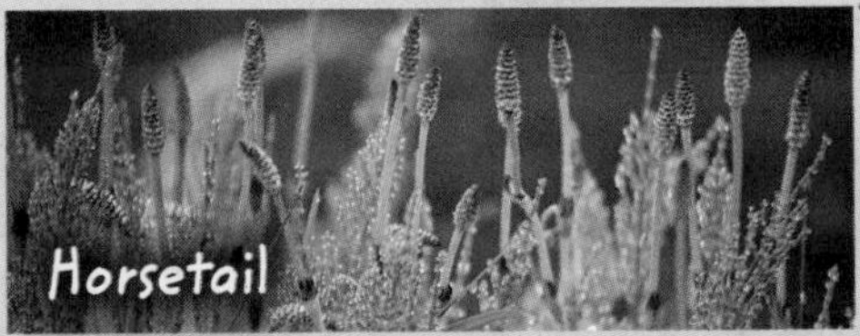
Horsetail

Seed vascular plants

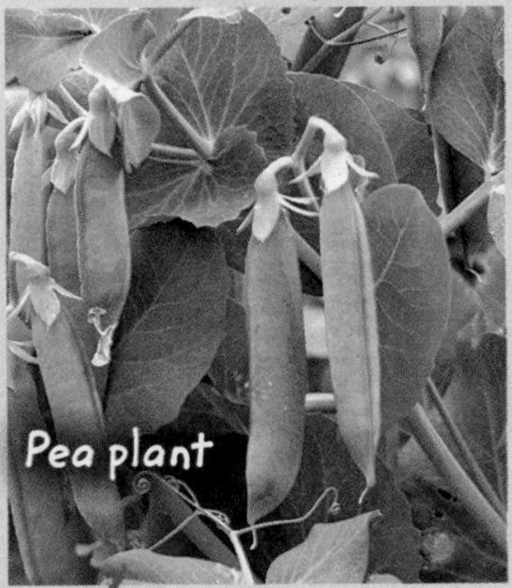
Pea plant

B Summarize the similarities and differences.

____

____

____

____

Gymnosperms (nonflowering plants)

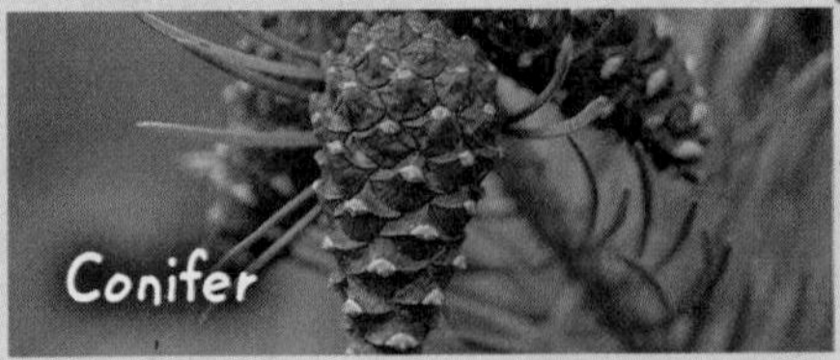
Conifer

Angiosperms (flowering plants)

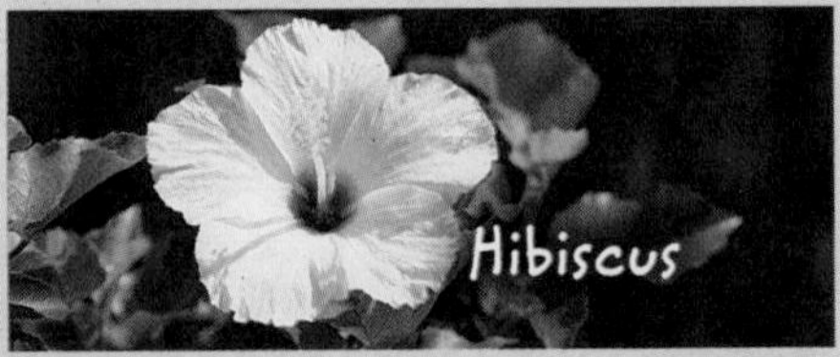
Hibiscus

C Summarize the similarities and differences.

____

____

____

Why It Matters

EYE ON THE ENVIRONMENT

Pharmaceuticals and Plants

Throughout history, plants have played an important role in medicine. Many modern medicines are derived from chemicals found in plants. Tropical rain forests are a source of many potential medicinal plants. For example, the cat's claw shown here is a woody vine found in the Amazon rain forest. It is used by local tribes to treat arthritis and some viral infections. Research is under way to find out if cat's claw might be useful for treating a variety of diseases. Scientists have discovered many useful compounds in rain-forest plants, and are likely to discover many more.

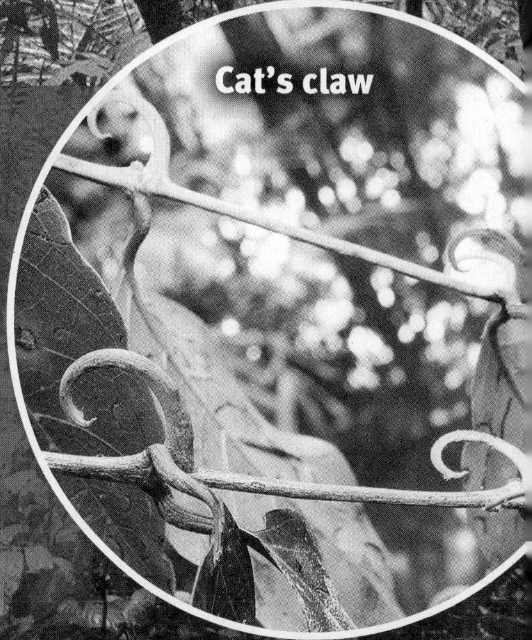
Cat's claw

White Willow Tree

The white willow tree is native to Europe and Asia. The medicinal value of white willow bark goes back to ancient Egyptians, who used white willow to treat inflammation. A compound in white willow, salicin, led to the development of aspirin.

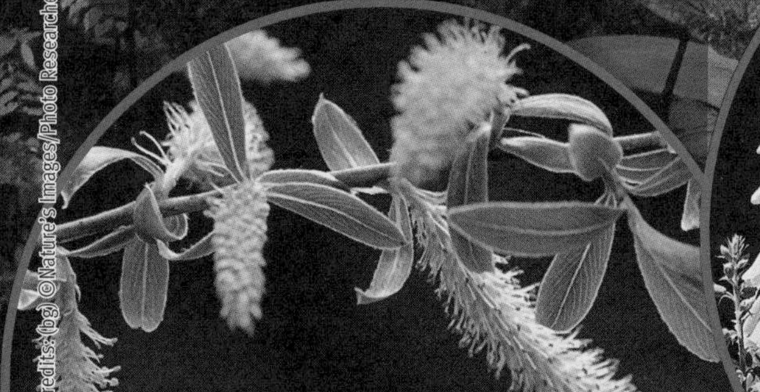

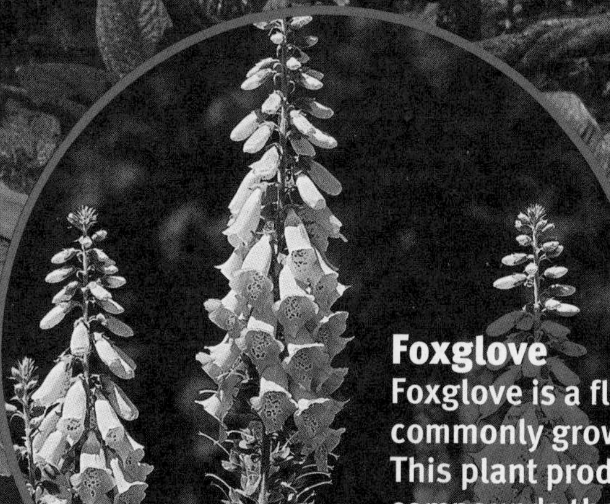

Foxglove

Foxglove is a flowering plant commonly grown in gardens. This plant produces uncommon compounds that are used to make medicine for the heart.

Extend

Inquiry

18 Summarize How are the compounds derived from the foxglove plant and the white willow tree used in medicine?

19 Research Find out how another plant is used in modern medicine.

20 Propose How can we protect medicinal plants in rain forests?

Visual Summary

To complete this summary, write at least two facts on each card about the groups of plants. Then, use the key below to check your answers. You can use this page to review the main concepts of the lesson.

Nonvascular plants do not have vessels to transport nutrients and water.

21 Summary points:

_____

_____

Seedless vascular plants have a vascular system, roots, and shoots, and reproduce using spores.

22 Summary points:

_____

_____

Introduction to Plants

A gymnosperm is a vascular seed plant whose seeds are not enclosed by fruit.

23 Summary points:

_____

_____

An angiosperm is a flowering, vascular seed plant whose seeds are enclosed within a fruit.

24 Summary points:

_____

_____

Sample answers: 21 can grow in harsh environments, spores, rhizoids. 22 have vascular tissue, roots, rhizomes, and spores. 23 vascular plants, produce seeds without fruit, produce pollen, produce cones. 24 produce seeds in fruit, produce flowers and pollen

25 Infer What characteristics of flowering plants have helped them to be successful?

Lesson Review

Vocabulary

Fill in the blank with the term that best completes the following sentence.

1 A(n) _____ is a plant organ that consists of an embryo, tissues, and a protective coating.

2 Most plants are called _____ because they can make their own food using photosynthesis.

3 Vascular plants that have seeds surrounded by fruit are called _____

Key Concepts

4 Identify What characteristics do all plants share?

_____

_____

_____

_____

_____

5 Summarize What is the importance of having a vascular system?

_____

_____

_____

_____

_____

6 Identify List the function of each of the following parts of a flower: stamen, pistil, ovary, and sepal.

_____

_____

_____

_____

_____

_____

_____

Critical Thinking

Use the image to answer the following questions.

7 Identify Which letter corresponds to the structure that absorbs water and minerals?

_____

8 Label Which letter corresponds to the part of the plant that is primarily used for photosynthesis?

_____

9 Infer Is this an example of a vascular plant? How do you know?

_____

_____

_____

10 Conclude A scientist discovers a new plant that has vascular tissue and produces seeds. It has brightly colored, scented flowers. What type of plant did the scientist discover? How might this plant be pollinated, and what would lead you to draw that conclusion?

_____

_____

_____

_____

_____

_____

My Notes

Plant Processes

ESSENTIAL QUESTION

How do plants stay alive?

By the end of this lesson, you should be able to describe the processes through which plants obtain energy, reproduce, and respond to their environments.

The Venus flytrap responds to touch. When the leaf is triggered by an insect, the trap snaps shut in 0.1 second!

 **Lesson Labs**

Quick Labs
• Investigating Plant Pigments
• Observing Stomata

Exploration Lab
• Fertilization in Angiosperms

Engage Your Brain

1 Identify Read over the following vocabulary terms. In the spaces provided, place a + if you know the term well, a – if you have heard the term but are not sure what it means, and a ? if you are unfamiliar with the term. Then write a sentence that includes one of the words you are most familiar with.

_____ cellular respiration

_____ transpiration

_____ tropism

_____ pollination

Sentence using known word:

_____

_____

_____

2 Describe Finish the caption for this photo.

The vine responds to the wire by

_____

_____

Active Reading

3 Synthesize You can often define an unknown word if you know the meaning of its word parts. Use the word parts and sentence below to make an educated guess about the meaning of the word *photosynthesis*.

Word part	Meaning
photo-	light
synthesis	putting together

Example sentence:
Plants die without sunlight because they are unable to carry out <u>photosynthesis</u>.

photosynthesis:

_____

_____

Vocabulary Terms

• cellular respiration
• pollination
• stamen
• pistil

• stimulus
• transpiration
• tropism
• dormant

4 Apply As you learn the definition of each vocabulary term in this lesson, create your own definition or sketch to help you remember the meaning of the term.

© Houghton Mifflin Harcourt Publishing Company • Image Credits: (bg) ©Alfred Pasieka/Science Photo Library; (tr) ©Michaela Dušková/Alamy Images

Fueled By the Sun

How do plants obtain and use energy?

Plants, like all living things, need energy to survive. But plants don't exactly "eat" to get energy. Plants get energy from sunlight during the process of photosynthesis.

Plants Capture Light Energy in Chloroplasts

Plants use photosynthesis to change light energy to chemical energy in the form of sugar. Unlike animal cells, plant cells have organelles called *chloroplasts* [KLOHR•uh•plasts], where photosynthesis takes place. Chloroplasts are made up of two membranes that surround stacks of smaller, circular membranes. These smaller membranes contain chlorophyll, which is a green pigment. Chlorophyll absorbs light energy from the sun.

Sunlight is made up of various wavelengths of light. Different wavelengths of visible light are seen as different colors. Chlorophyll absorbs many wavelengths, but it reflects more green light than other colors of light. As a result, most plants look green.

Visualize It!

5 Describe Fill in the captions to describe how plants obtain energy from sunlight.

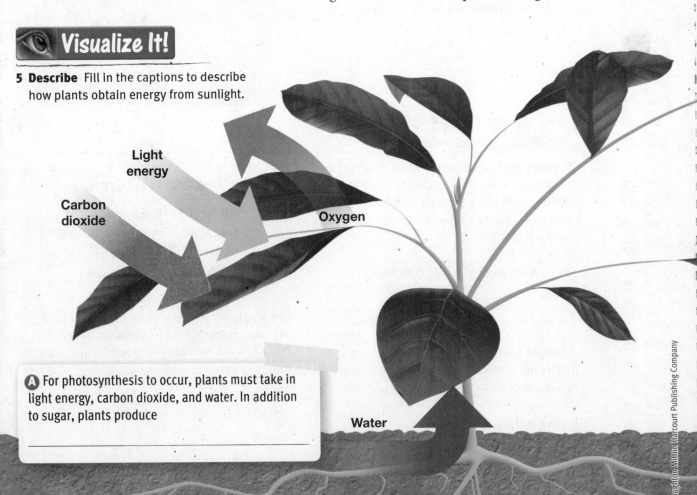

Light energy

Carbon dioxide

Oxygen

Water

A For photosynthesis to occur, plants must take in light energy, carbon dioxide, and water. In addition to sugar, plants produce

_____

Chloroplasts Use Light Energy to Make Sugar

The light energy captured in chloroplasts is changed and stored in the bonds of a sugar called glucose. In the same process, oxygen gas is released. Many chemical reactions occur during photosynthesis. The process can be summarized by the following equation:

Photosynthesis

$$6CO_2 + 6H_2O \xrightarrow{\text{light energy}} C_6H_{12}O_6 + 6O_2$$

This equation shows that light energy is used to change six molecules of carbon dioxide and six molecules of water into one molecule of glucose and six molecules of oxygen gas.

Mitochondria Release Energy from Sugar

In plants, extra glucose is stored as starch or changed to other types of sugar such as fructose or sucrose. **Cellular respiration** [SEL•yuh•luhr res•puh•RAY•shun] is the process by which cells use oxygen to release the stored energy from the bonds of sugar molecules. This process occurs in mitochondria. Cellular respiration also produces carbon dioxide and water.

Cellular respiration

$$C_6H_{12}O_6 + 6O_2 \longrightarrow 6CO_2 + 6H_2O + energy$$

In cellular respiration, one molecule of glucose and six molecules of oxygen are changed into six molecules of carbon dioxide and six molecules of water. The reaction changes the energy in sugar into energy that can be used to power cell processes.

6 Relate How is cellular respiration the reverse of photosynthesis?

_____

_____

_____

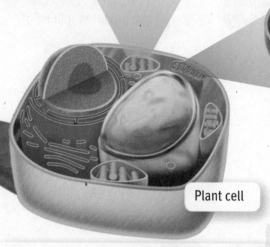

Chloroplast

Plant cell

B Plant cells have organelles called chloroplasts, where photosynthesis takes place. These organelles contain a pigment called

_____

that absorbs light.

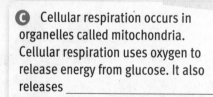

Mitochondrion

C Cellular respiration occurs in organelles called mitochondria. Cellular respiration uses oxygen to release energy from glucose. It also releases _____

and _____

A Plant's Life

What are the phases of a plant's life cycle?

All plants complete their life cycles by alternating between two phases, the sporophyte phase and the gametophyte phase. These two phases look different from each other.

In one phase, plants called sporophytes [SPOHR•uh•fyts] produce spores by meiosis. Meiosis is a process of cell division in which each daughter cell receives half the chromosomes of the parent cell. The products of meiosis in plant sporophytes are spores. The spores are then released.

Under the right conditions, spores grow into plants called gametophytes [guh•MEET•uh•fyts]. Female gametophytes make eggs. Male gametophytes make sperm. When a sperm fertilizes an egg, they combine to form an embryo. The embryo develops into a seed, which is released and can grow into a new sporophyte.

Visualize It!

7 Contrast Use the diagram to explain how spores differ from seeds.

_____

_____

_____

sporophyte

In the sporophyte phase, a seed grows into a plant that produces spores.

seed

A sperm and an egg combine to produce a seed.

Spores are produced.

sperm **eggs**

spores

Sperm and eggs are produced.

In the gametophyte phase, spores grow into plants that produce eggs and sperm.

gametophyte

Fern sporophytes

© Houghton Mifflin Harcourt Publishing Company • Image Credits: ©Corbis

How do seedless plants reproduce?

The gametophyte generation in plants makes eggs and sperm. In seedless plants, sperm are released in the presence of water. Sperm have whip-like tails. The sperm swim to the eggs and fertilize them. The fertilized eggs then grow into sporophytes.

Some seedless plants, such as mosses, have a visible gametophyte phase. The short, dense plant you think of as moss is the gametophyte. Sometimes you can also see the sporophytes of moss if you look closely. They are thin, brown stems topped by a small, brown capsule.

How do seed plants reproduce?

The sporophyte is what you see in seed plants. In most seed plants, the sporophyte makes two types of spores, male and female, that grow into microscopic male and female gametophytes. The male gametophyte is pollen, a tiny structure in which sperm form. Pollen may be carried by wind, water, or animals to the female plant reproductive structure. The female gametophyte develops inside an ovule, which is part of the sporophyte. Within the ovule the gametophyte produces eggs. **Pollination** happens when pollen lands on the female plant reproductive structure and fertilizes the eggs. The fertilized egg develops into an embryo and the ovule becomes the seed.

Moss

Sporophytes

Gametophyte

In a conifer, the male gametophyte (pollen) forms inside the male cone.

Sporophyte

The female gametophyte forms inside the female cone.

8 Diagram Fill in the Venn diagram to compare and contrast the way seedless and seed plants reproduce.

Reproduction of seedless plants   *Both*   *Reproduction of seed plants*

How do flowering plants reproduce?

In flowering plants, sexual reproduction takes place inside the flowers. Flowers are reproductive structures that have specialized leaves called sepals and petals, which often attract animal pollinators such as insects.

A **stamen** is the male reproductive structure of flowers. At the tip of each stamen is an *anther,* where pollen is produced. A **pistil** is the female reproductive structure of flowers. When a pollen grain reaches the tip of the pistil, called the *stigma,* pollination occurs. A pollen tube grows down through the pistil into the ovary. Within the ovary are one or more ovules containing eggs. Sperm travel down the tube, into the ovary, and fertilize the eggs.

A fertilized egg develops into an embryo, a tiny, undeveloped plant. The ovule develops into a seed that surrounds and protects the embryo. The ovary becomes a fruit, which protects the seeds and helps seeds to spread. When conditions are right, seeds will sprout and grow into new plants.

Visualize It!

9 Identify Circle the two labels of gametophyte structures in the illustration.

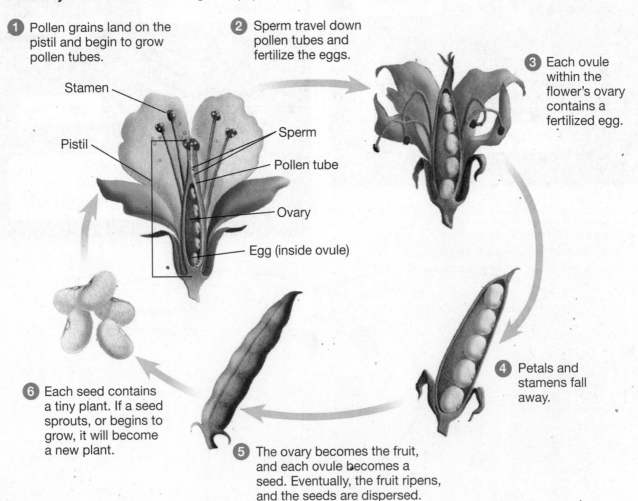

1 Pollen grains land on the pistil and begin to grow pollen tubes.

2 Sperm travel down pollen tubes and fertilize the eggs.

3 Each ovule within the flower's ovary contains a fertilized egg.

Stamen

Pistil

Sperm

Pollen tube

Ovary

Egg (inside ovule)

4 Petals and stamens fall away.

5 The ovary becomes the fruit, and each ovule becomes a seed. Eventually, the fruit ripens, and the seeds are dispersed.

6 Each seed contains a tiny plant. If a seed sprouts, or begins to grow, it will become a new plant.

How do plants reproduce asexually?

Most plants can also reproduce asexually. Asexual reproduction allows a plant to reproduce without seeds or spores. During asexual reproduction, part of a parent plant, such as a stem or root, produces a new plant. Some examples of structures that plants use to reproduce asexually include plantlets, tubers, and runners.

- Plantlets are tiny plants that grow along the edges of a plant's leaves. These plantlets fall off and grow on their own.
- Tubers are underground stems that store nutrients and can grow into new plants. A potato is a tuber. Each "eye" can grow into a new plant.
- Runners are above-ground stems that can grow into new plants. Strawberries send out lots of runners.

Think Outside the Book Inquiry

11 **Apply** Write a play that compares and contrasts the results of sexual and asexual reproduction in plants.

Visualize It!

10 Label Under each example of asexual reproduction, write the type of structure used for this purpose.

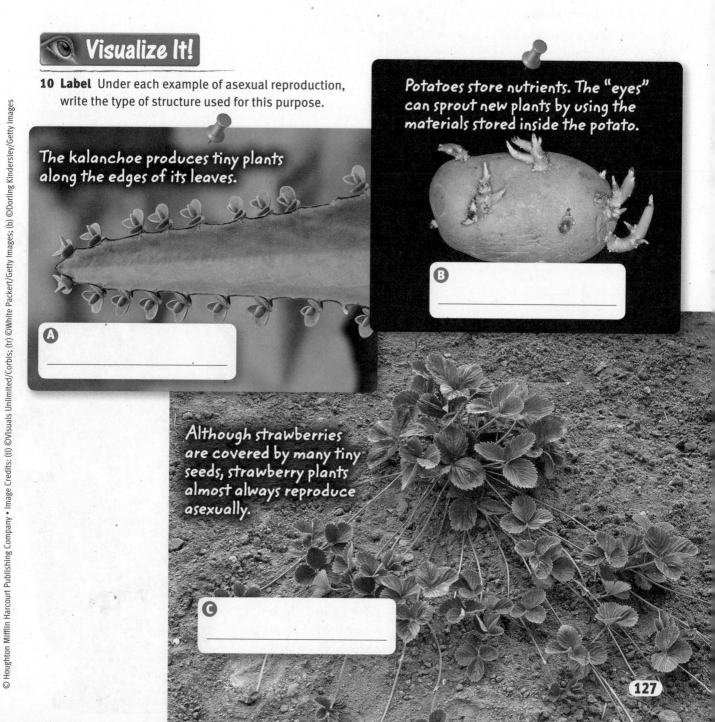

The kalanchoe produces tiny plants along the edges of its leaves.

A _____

Potatoes store nutrients. The "eyes" can sprout new plants by using the materials stored inside the potato.

B _____

Although strawberries are covered by many tiny seeds, strawberry plants almost always reproduce asexually.

C _____

Action, Reaction

What are some ways plants respond to their environment?

Anything that causes a reaction or change in an organism is a **stimulus**. Plants can respond to internal stimuli, such as water levels in cells. Plants can also respond to external stimuli, such as the amount of light they receive.

By Wilting

A stoma (plural, stomata) is an opening in the surface of a leaf. Stomata help a plant exchange gases and respond to its water levels. Each stoma is surrounded by two guard cells that open and close the stoma. When stomata are open, carbon dioxide enters the leaf, and oxygen and water vapor exit the leaf. The loss of water from leaves is called **transpiration**. A plant wilts when it loses more water than it can absorb through its roots. When a plant is wilting, its stomata close, preventing further water loss.

12 **Infer** Why are plant stomata usually open during the day?

_____

_____

_____

These stomata are greatly magnified. Color has been added to the images so the openings can be seen more clearly.

When stomata are open, plants can obtain carbon dioxide for photosynthesis and get rid of extra oxygen. They also lose water vapor.

When plants lose more water than they absorb, they wilt.

By Growing

Plant growth in response to a stimulus is called a **tropism**. Plant tropisms are controlled by plant hormones. Hormones are chemical messengers that cause changes in cells.

A change in the direction of plant growth in response to light is called phototropism [foh•toh•TROH•piz•uhm], as shown in the photo on the left. Hormones build up in cells on the shaded side of the stem, causing these cells to lengthen. The lengthening of these cells makes the stem bend in the direction of the light.

A change in the direction of plant growth in response to gravity is called gravitropism [grav•ih•TROH•piz•uhm], shown on the right. Most stems grow upward, away from the pull of Earth's gravity, and most roots grow downward, toward the pull of gravity.

 **Active Reading**

13 Identify As you read, underline the effect of phototropism.

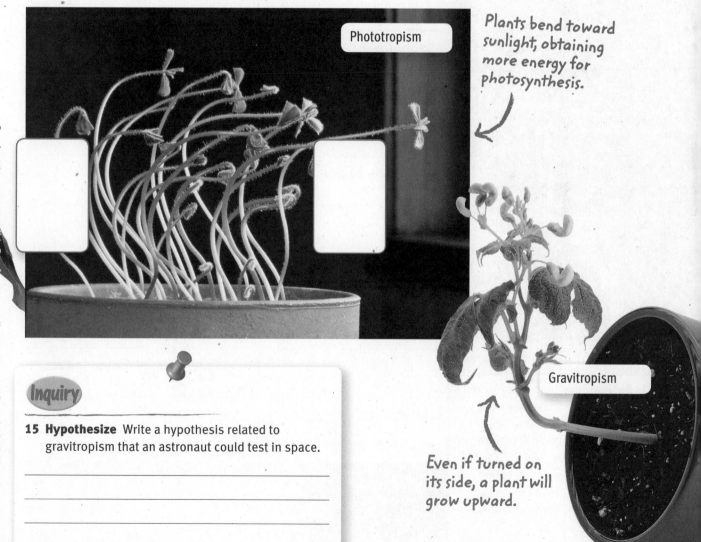

Visualize It!

14 Label Draw an X next to the side of the stems with shorter cells.

Phototropism

Plants bend toward sunlight, obtaining more energy for photosynthesis.

Gravitropism

Even if turned on its side, a plant will grow upward.

Inquiry

15 Hypothesize Write a hypothesis related to gravitropism that an astronaut could test in space.

By Going Dormant

The difference between day length and night length is an important stimulus for many plants. Shorter days and longer nights during fall help trigger winter dormancy. **Dormant** describes the inactive state of a seed or other plant part when conditions are not right for growth. For many plants, it is more energy-efficient to shut down during winter, or during a dry season, than to continue photosynthesis under conditions of reduced sunlight and rain. These plants survive by living off of stored sugars.

Many plants and seeds come out of dormancy in the spring. Their growth is triggered by the return of more direct sunlight, longer daylight hours, and increased rain. Each plant species has an ideal temperature at which most of its seeds begin to grow. For many plants, this is about 27 °C (80 °F). But some seeds need extreme conditions, such as forest fires, to break their dormancy.

16 Summarize Use the filled in boxes as clues to help you complete the table with information from the lesson. Some terms will appear more than once.

Stimulus	Response
	closing stomata to preserve water
	growth of roots downward
direction of light	
touch	growth of stem around a wire
	growth of stems upward
	seed growth
	changing leaf color, losing leaves
forest fire	

As a tree prepares to go dormant, the supply of nutrients to its leaves are shut off. Green chlorophyll breaks down first, revealing orange or yellow pigments in the leaves. Eventually, the leaves fall off and the tree goes dormant.

Think Outside the Book Inquiry

17 Design Tulip bulbs are planted in the fall because they must go dormant in order to bloom the next spring. They require temperatures below 7 °C (45 °F). Design an experiment to find out how long tulip bulbs must remain in the cold dormant state before blooming.

130

In Season

Like all plants, our food plants also respond to seasons. The growing season occurs when temperature, light, and water conditions favor growth for that type of plant. You may not know what the growing season is for many common fruits and vegetables, because out-of-season produce is almost always available in stores. These foods are grown in a greenhouse or in other parts of the world and then shipped to your store.

Spring

Artichokes are the immature flowers of the artichoke plant. Artichokes are in season in the spring.

Winter

Broccoli are the flower buds of a broccoli plant. Most varieties of broccoli are considered winter vegetables and can withstand frost.

Summer

Tomatoes are the ripened ovaries, or fruits, of the tomato plant. Tomato plants need a lot of light. When tomatoes are ripened in storage, they appear lighter in color and have a different texture than tomatoes ripened in sunlight.

Fall

Pumpkins, squashes, and gourds are grown on vines. Pumpkins are part of fall traditions in the U.S. because they are in season in the fall.

Extend

Inquiry

18 Relate All of the plants shown here are seed plants. Which phase of the life cycle do you see?

19 Research Learn the growing season of five fruits or vegetables that are grown in your state.

20 Apply Plan a menu for a meal that uses three of the fruits and vegetables that you learned about that all become ripe in the same season.

Visual Summary

To complete this summary, circle the correct word. Then, use the key below to check your answers. You can use this page to review the main concepts of the lesson.

Plant Processes

During photosynthesis, plants use energy from sunlight to make food out of carbon dioxide and water.

Light energy
Carbon dioxide
Oxygen
Water

21 Photosynthesis takes place in chloroplasts / mitochondria, which contain chlorophyll.

22 Photosynthesis / cellular respiration releases the energy stored in food and produces carbon dioxide and water.

Plants respond to environmental stimuli such as light, gravity, and changing seasons.

25 Growth, wilting, and dormancy are examples of plant responses / stimuli.

Plants complete their life cycles by alternating between sporophytes and gametophytes.

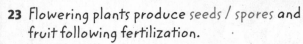

23 Flowering plants produce seeds / spores and fruit following fertilization.

24 Some plants use plantlets, tubers, or runners to reproduce sexually / asexually.

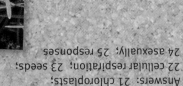

26 **Explain** What are two ways in which photosynthesis is important?

Lesson Review

Vocabulary

Fill in the blank with the term that best completes the following sentence.

1 _____ is the transfer of pollen from the male reproductive structures to the female structures of seed plants.

2 The process by which plants release water vapor into the air through stomata is called

_____

3 A _____ is the female reproductive structure of flowers.

4 Seeds are _____ when conditions are unfavorable for growth.

Key Concepts

5 Identify Explain what a plant produces in each of the two parts of its life cycle.

_____

_____

6 List Provide three examples of asexual plant structures.

_____

_____

_____

7 Predict In which parts of a plant would you expect phototropism to occur? Explain.

_____

_____

_____

8 Explain Describe the roles of chloroplasts and chlorophyll in photosynthesis.

_____

_____

_____

Critical Thinking

Use this graph to answer the following questions.

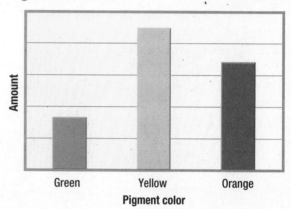

Pigments In Leaves

9 Analyze What external stimuli produced the results shown in the graph above?

_____

_____

10 Conclude Based on the graph, what process has slowed down? Explain how you know this.

_____

_____

_____

_____

11 Synthesize Can an organism carry out cellular respiration without photosynthesis? How about photosynthesis without cellular respiration? Explain.

_____

_____

_____

_____

_____

_____

My Notes

Evaluating Technological Systems

Skills
✓ Identify inputs
✓ Identify outputs
✓ Identify system processes
✓ Identify system feedback
Examine system interactions
Apply system controls
✓ Communicate results

Objectives
• Identify inputs and outputs of a physical system.
• Differentiate between convective and radiative heat transfer.
• Graph temperature data versus time.
• Analyze and communicate results of an experiment.

Analyzing a Greenhouse

A greenhouse is an enclosed space that maintains a consistent environment and temperature to let people grow plants where the natural climate is not ideal. A greenhouse system needs to heat up and cool off in order to effectively grow plants. How the sun warms a greenhouse involves both radiation and convection. Objects on the ground absorb sunlight and become warm. At the same time, objects cool off primarily in two ways: (1) they get rid of heat by transferring energy as visible light or infrared (in•fruh•RED) light (radiation), or (2) they transfer energy in the form of heat to the air, which then carries it away (convection). A greenhouse retains energy in the form of heat primarily because its roof and walls prevent its warmed air from moving out into the atmosphere.

1 Infer Identify the processes shown at labels A and B as either convection or radiation.

A _____

B _____

Infer Why is convection the main process regulating the temperature in a greenhouse?

_____

_____

_____

_____

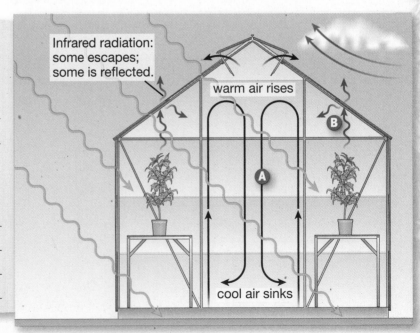

Infrared radiation: some escapes; some is reflected.

warm air rises

cool air sinks

Greenhouse Systems

Greenhouses are systems that have inputs and outputs. The inputs are air, water, sunlight, young plants or seeds, and plant nutrients. The outputs are energy in the form of heat and mature plants, fruits, or vegetables. The main uses of greenhouses are agriculture (farming) and horticulture (HOHR•tih•kuhl•cher) (gardening). Typical outputs of agricultural greenhouses are fruits and vegetables. Typical outputs of horticultural greenhouses are ornamental plants and flowers. Greenhouses can vary in size from very large to the size of a shoebox. Gardeners call small greenhouses *cold frames.*

2 Infer Three different types of greenhouses are shown here. Label each type of greenhouse agriculture, horticulture, or cold frame, and list the likely outputs of each.

A
_____
_____

B
_____
_____

C
_____
_____

✋ **You Try It!** ⟶

Now it's your turn to make a greenhouse and analyze how it works.

 # You Try It!

Now it's your turn to construct a mini-greenhouse and analyze its inputs, how it heats up, and how its temperature is regulated.

You Will Need

✓ small box, 8 in. (length) x 5 in. (width) x 3 in. (height)

✓ thermometer, digital if possible (1)

✓ marking pens, brown or black

✓ clear plastic wrap

✓ tape or rubber bands

✓ aluminum foil

✓ lamp

(1) Identify Inputs

What are the inputs of your greenhouse?

_____

_____

(2) Identify Outputs

What are the outputs of your greenhouse?

_____

_____

(3) Identify System Processes

A First, record the room-temperature reading of your thermometer. _____

B Then, begin to construct your greenhouse using the materials listed. With a marking pen, color the inside of your box to simulate the color of dirt.

C Place your thermometer in the box so that it does not touch any part of the box but so that you can still read it. Why should the thermometer not touch the box?

_____

_____

_____

D Using the foil, make a tent-style barrier in the box to shade the thermometer so the lamp does not directly shine on it. Why is it important to shade the thermometer?

_____

_____

_____

E Cover the box with clear plastic wrap, and seal it as best you can with tape or a rubber band to minimize air leaks. Place the lamp above the box to act as the sun.

F What physical processes are involved in your greenhouse system as it accumulates heat energy?

_____

_____

_____

_____

④ Identify System Feedbacks

Record the temperature of the air in the greenhouse every 5 minutes for at least 30 minutes. Add scale values on tick marks to both axes. Then, graph the temperature versus time in the space provided.

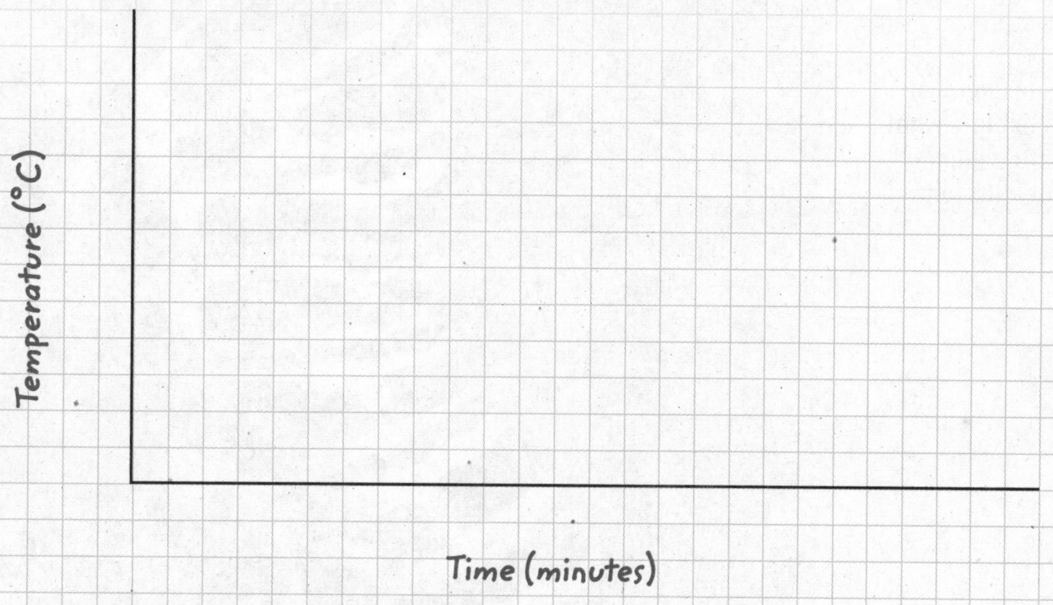

Temperature (°C) vs. Time (minutes)

⑤ Communicate Results

Describe what you learned from your greenhouse experiment.

_____

_____

_____

_____

_____

Introduction to Animals

ESSENTIAL QUESTION

What are animals?

By the end of this lesson, you should be able to explain what characteristics define animals, and describe some different kinds of animals.

Animals come in many different sizes and shapes. Scientists have identified more than 1 million living species of animals.

Engage Your Brain

1 Predict Check T or F to show whether you think each statement is true or false.

T F

☐ ☐ Animals are producers because they can make their own food.

☐ ☐ An invertebrate is an animal that does not have a backbone.

☐ ☐ Sponges are classified as animals.

☐ ☐ Birds are more closely related to mammals than to reptiles.

2 Compare What do the two kinds of animals shown here have in common?

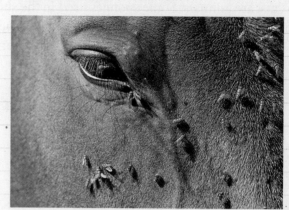

_____

_____

_____

Active Reading

3 Synthesize You can often define an unknown word if you know the meaning of its word parts. Use the word parts and sentences below to make an educated guess about the meaning of the words *exoskeleton* and *endoskeleton*.

Word part	Meaning
exo-	outer, external
endo-	inner, internal
skeleton	framework

Example sentence:
An insect is covered by a hard <u>exoskeleton</u>.

exoskeleton

_____

Example sentence:
The <u>endoskeleton</u> of a bird is made of bone.

endoskeleton

_____

Vocabulary Terms

• consumer
• invertebrate
• exoskeleton
• vertebrate
• endoskeleton

4 Apply As you learn the definition of each vocabulary term in this lesson, create your own definition or sketch to help you remember the meaning of the term.

You Are an Animal!

What characteristics do animals share?

Animals come in many shapes and sizes. Pets, such as dogs and cats, are animals. Some sponges used in the shower are the remains of an animal. Some animals are too small to be seen without a microscope. Yet all animals share six characteristics.

Many Cells

Like other organisms, animals are made up of cells. All animals are *multicellular* organisms, which means that they are made up of many cells. Similar cells work together to perform the animal's life functions. Animal cells are eukaryotic, so they have a nucleus. In animals, all of the cells work together to perform the life functions of the animal.

Specialized Parts

The cells in a multicellular organism develop into different kinds of cells. This process is called differentiation. Some cells may become skin cells, and others may become gut cells. Each type of cell has a special function to play in an organism. For example, retinal cells of the eye function in vision.

Visualize It!

5 Infer These photos show different kinds of animal cells. Write down three other specialized cells that you think would be found in animal bodies.

_____

_____

_____

Cell differentiation leads to different kinds of cells. Each type of cell performs a specific function in the animal.

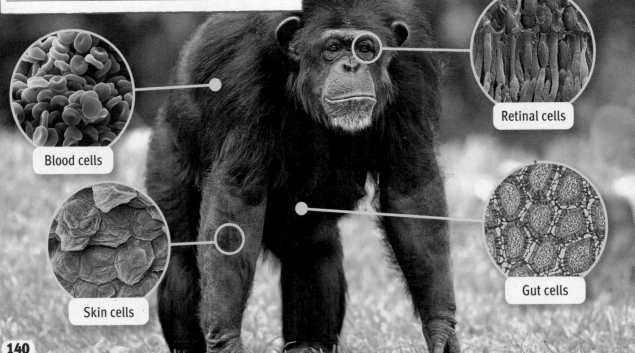

Blood cells

Skin cells

Retinal cells

Gut cells

Movement

Animals move in various ways such as running, flying, and swimming. Some animals move to find food, shelter, and mates. Some animals move during only part of their life cycle. For example, the immature stage of a barnacle, the larva, swims around to find food. But adult barnacles are permanently attached to a hard surface, such as a rock, and catch food that passes by.

Reproduction

Most animals use sexual reproduction. In sexual reproduction, a male sex cell, the sperm, fertilizes a female sex cell, the egg. Then the fertilized egg, or zygote, divides many times to form an embryo. Sexual reproduction leads to genetically diverse offspring. Some animals, such as hydras and sponges, can also reproduce asexually. Offspring of asexual reproduction are genetically identical to their parent.

Consume Food

Active Reading **6 Identify** As you read, underline the different kinds of food animals eat.

All organisms need energy to survive. Animals cannot produce their own food, so they are consumers. A **consumer** is an animal that eats other organisms, or parts of organisms, to get the energy it needs for life processes. Animals eat many kinds of food. Some animals eat plants, some eat animals or animal products, and some eat both plants and animals.

Maintain Body Temperature

To function well, all animals need to maintain their bodies within a specific range of temperatures. Birds and mammals maintain their own body temperatures by using some of the energy released by chemical reactions. Other animals rely on their environment to maintain their body temperature.

Some animals, like barnacles, can move from place to place only during the early larval stage of their life cycle.

Adult barnacles

Barnacle larva

Some animals have specialized diets. South American vampire bats feed only on blood.

7 Infer How might an organism that relies on the environment to maintain body temperature do so?

_____

_____

_____

_____

Such Diversity!

What groups make up the diversity of animals?

Animals live in nearly every ecosystem on Earth. They are the most physically diverse kingdom of organisms. Some animals have four legs and some have none. Others, like rotifers, are smaller than the period ending this sentence. Blue whales are as big as two school buses! Besides shape and size, animals have body coverings that vary from feathers to hard shells to soft tissues.

One way to categorize animals is by symmetry or body plan. Some animals, such as sponges, are asymmetrical. You cannot draw a straight line to divide its body into equal parts. Animals like the sea anemone have a radial body plan, organized like the spokes of a wheel. Animals such as tortoises have bilateral symmetry with two mirror-image sides. Animals can also be categorized by internal traits, such as whether or not they have a backbone.

Body Plans

Asymmetry In asymmetry, the animal is irregular in shape and, therefore, lacks symmetry.

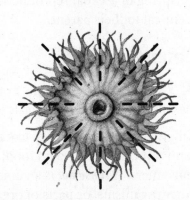

Radial symmetry The bodies of animals with radial symmetry are organized like spokes on a wheel.

Bilateral symmetry Animals with bilateral symmetry have two sides that mirror each other along one plane through the central axis.

Outer Coverings

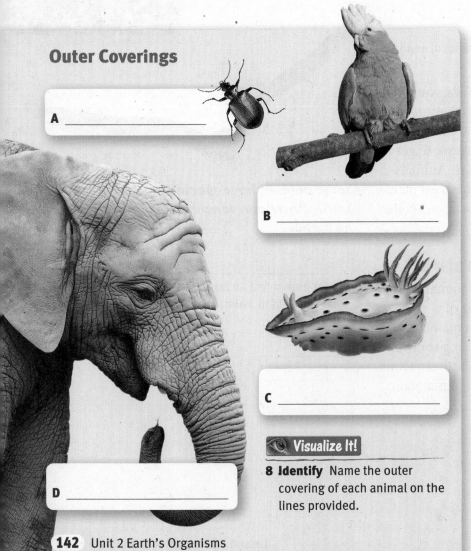

A _____

B _____

C _____

D _____

> **◉ Visualize It!**
>
> **8 Identify** Name the outer covering of each animal on the lines provided.

Invertebrates

An **invertebrate** is an animal without a backbone. In fact, invertebrates do not have any bones. Instead, many invertebrates have a hard, external covering, which supports the body, called an **exoskeleton**. Most animals on Earth—over 95% of all animal species—are invertebrates.

Asexual reproduction is more common in invertebrates than in other animals. For example, the phyla that include animals such as sponges, jellyfish, flatworms, and segmented worms use both sexual and asexual reproduction.

Two special kinds of invertebrates are tunicates and lancelets. Tunicates, such as sea squirts, are small, sac-shaped animals. Lancelets are small, fish-shaped animals as shown below. These invertebrate animals are unique because they share some characteristics with vertebrates.

Vertebrates

Tunicates and lancelets, along with vertebrates, are part of a group of animals called *chordates* (KOHR•dayts). Chordates have four traits at some point in their life: a notochord, a hollow nerve cord, pharyngeal (fuh•RIN•jee•uhl) slits, and a tail.

Animals that have a backbone are called **vertebrates**. The backbone is a part of an endoskeleton. An **endoskeleton** is an internal skeleton that supports an animal's body. The backbone is made up of bones called *vertebrae* (VER•tuh•bray) that protect part of the nervous system. Vertebrates also have a braincase, or skull, that protects their large brains. Almost all vertebrates reproduce sexually. In a few species, a female's egg can develop into an individual without being fertilized.

Visualize It!

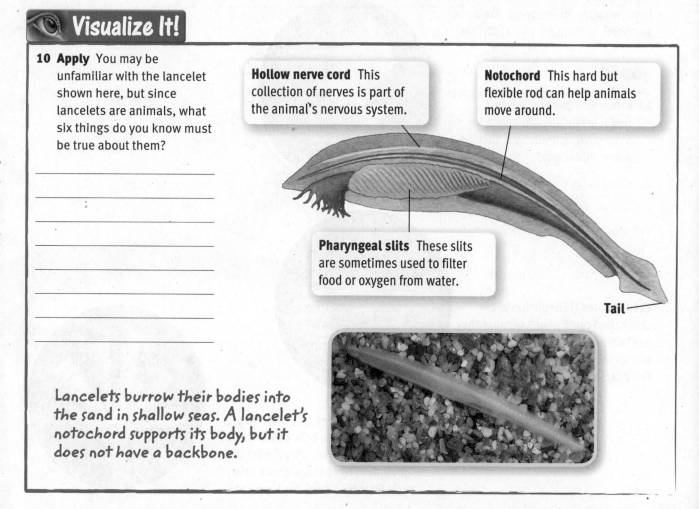

10 Apply You may be unfamiliar with the lancelet shown here, but since lancelets are animals, what six things do you know must be true about them?

_____

_____

_____

_____

_____

_____

Hollow nerve cord This collection of nerves is part of the animal's nervous system.

Notochord This hard but flexible rod can help animals move around.

Pharyngeal slits These slits are sometimes used to filter food or oxygen from water.

Tail

Lancelets burrow their bodies into the sand in shallow seas. A lancelet's notochord supports its body, but it does not have a backbone.

Soft and Squishy?

What are some different kinds of invertebrates?

Most animal species are invertebrates. The figure shows some of the vast diversity of animals that make up this group. Scientists once used only structural characteristics to classify animals. Today, scientists also use DNA to place animals into groups related by their evolutionary history.

 Active Reading 11 **Identify** As you read the captions, underline the kind of environment where each group of invertebrates lives.

Invertebrate chordates

Echinoderms (ih•KY•nuh•dermz), such as sand dollars, live in oceans. Their endoskeleton has plates with spines, and a water vascular system helps them move. They have a complete digestive system.

Cnidarians (ny•DAIR•ee•uhnz) sting prey with their tentacles. They live in oceans and have two body forms: polyp, like a sea anemone, or medusa, like a jellyfish.

Inquiry

12 **Infer** Why might stinging tentacles be advantageous for slow-moving predators, such as some cnidarians?

_____
_____
_____
_____

Ctenophores (TEN•uh•fohrz) are also called comb jellies because they use comb-like rows of cilia on their bodies to move around. Comb jellies live only in marine environments.

Porifera includes sponges. They have specialized cells connected by jelly-like material, spend most of their lives fixed to the ocean floor, and filter food particles from water.

© Houghton Mifflin Harcourt Publishing Company • Image Credits: (t) Purple sea urchin Strongylocentrotus purpuratus : ©Mark Conlin/Alamy Images; (t) ©Picture Partners/Alamy Images; (b) ©Wolfgang Poezer/Alamy Images; (b) ©Charles V. Angelo/Photo Researchers, Inc.

Arthropoda (ar•THRAHP•uh•duh) includes animals that live on land and in water. They have jointed appendages and an exoskeleton that protects them from predators and prevents drying out.

Annelida includes segmented worms that live on land and in the ocean. Earthworms break down dead organisms in the soil. Some marine annelids filter food from the water.

Mollusca live in water or on land, and have soft bodies. Many, such as snails and clams, have a protective outer shell and a muscular foot. Squids have complex eyes.

Nematoda are roundworms. They live in fresh water, soil, or other animals. Many of these animals, such as hookworms, are parasites that cause disease.

Platyhelminthes (plat•ih•hel•MIN•theez), such as planaria, flukes, and tapeworms, are the simplest worms. Parasitic flatworms have simple tissues and a head with eyespots.

Think Outside the Book

13 Apply On your way home from school, write a list of all the invertebrate animals you see. Then do research to try to classify each one.

Some Familiar Faces...

What are some different kinds of vertebrates?

Vertebrates are divided into five main groups: fish, amphibians, reptiles, birds, and mammals. Vertebrates live in water, on land, or in both places. Some eat only plants, only animals, or both plants and animals. Today, both DNA and body form and structure are used to classify vertebrates.

Active Reading **14 Identify** As you read the captions, underline how vertebrates reproduce.

Reptiles have bodies covered with scales or plates, and reproduce by laying eggs. Examples of reptiles include turtles, snakes, lizards, and crocodiles. Reptiles can live nearly anywhere on land because they can lay eggs out of the water. Their eggs are protected from drying out by membranes and shells.

Amphibians live both on land and in water. Most amphibians have four limbs. Most live near fresh water because their eggs and larvae need water to survive. Also, all amphibians have thin skins that must be kept moist. Frogs, toads, and salamanders are examples of amphibians.

15 Relate What is the difference between an invertebrate chordate and a vertebrate chordate?

_____

_____

_____

_____

Invertebrate chordates

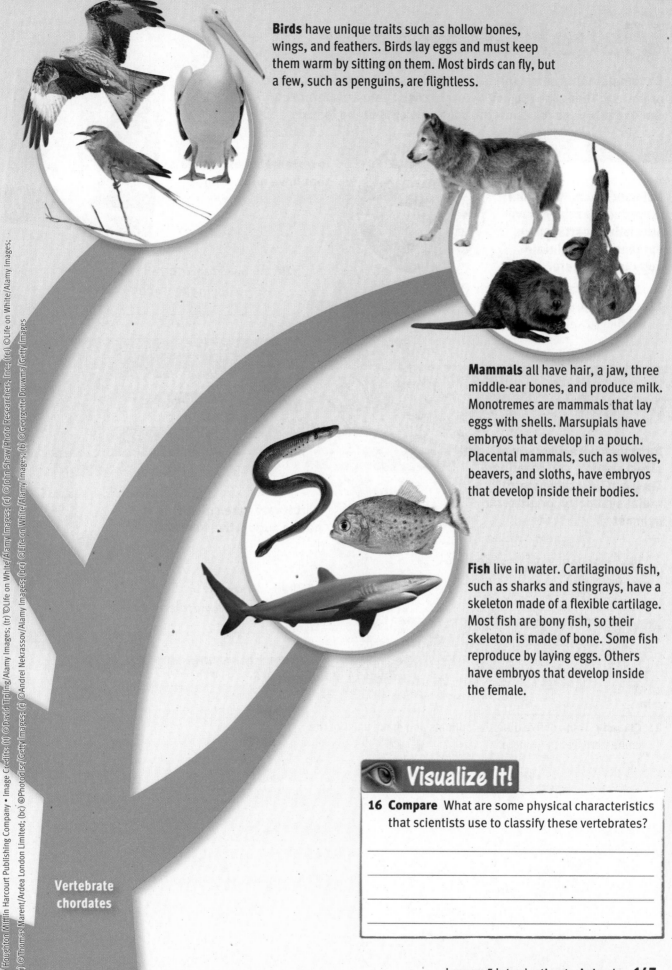

Birds have unique traits such as hollow bones, wings, and feathers. Birds lay eggs and must keep them warm by sitting on them. Most birds can fly, but a few, such as penguins, are flightless.

Mammals all have hair, a jaw, three middle-ear bones, and produce milk. Monotremes are mammals that lay eggs with shells. Marsupials have embryos that develop in a pouch. Placental mammals, such as wolves, beavers, and sloths, have embryos that develop inside their bodies.

Fish live in water. Cartilaginous fish, such as sharks and stingrays, have a skeleton made of a flexible cartilage. Most fish are bony fish, so their skeleton is made of bone. Some fish reproduce by laying eggs. Others have embryos that develop inside the female.

Vertebrate chordates

Visualize It!

16 Compare What are some physical characteristics that scientists use to classify these vertebrates?

_____

_____

_____

_____

Visual Summary

To complete this summary, fill in the blank with the correct word or phrase. Then, use the key below to check your answers. You can use this page to review the main concepts of the lesson.

Animals are multicellular, reproduce sexually, have specialized parts, move, eat food, and maintain body temperature.

17 An organism that gets energy by eating other organisms is a(n) _____

Invertebrates are animals that have no backbone.

19 An invertebrate that hunts prey with stinging tentacles is a(n) _____

Introduction to Animals

Animals have a diversity of sizes, shapes, and coverings. They can have asymmetry, radial symmetry, or bilateral symmetry.

18 An animal with two identical sides has _____ symmetry.

Vertebrates are animals that have a supportive backbone.

20 A skeleton that is inside the body and attaches to muscles is called a(n) _____

Answers: 17 consumer; 18 bilateral; 19 cnidarian; 20 endoskeleton

21 Classify Think of five different animals and make a list of the characteristics they share.

Lesson Review

Vocabulary

Fill in the blank with the term that best completes the following sentence.

1 _____ are organisms with a backbone.

2 Tunicates and lancelets are classified as _____ chordates.

3 The hard external covering of some invertebrates is called an _____.

Key Concepts

4 Identify List the six characteristics that animals share.

_____

_____

_____

_____

_____

5 Explain How do tunicates and lancelets differ from other chordates?

_____

_____

_____

_____

_____

6 Compare What is the major difference between invertebrates and vertebrates?

_____

_____

7 Identify What are two unique characteristics shared by all birds?

_____

_____

_____

Critical Thinking

Use the diagram to answer the following questions.

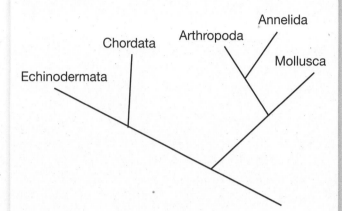

8 Analyze Which groups shown on the tree include invertebrates? Explain.

_____

_____

_____

9 Infer Do any of the groups shown on this tree include vertebrates? Explain.

_____

_____

_____

_____

10 Conclude Assess what kinds of traits make invertebrates such a diverse group of animals.

_____

_____

_____

_____

_____

_____

My Notes

Animal Behavior

ESSENTIAL QUESTION

What are some different animal behaviors?

By the end of this lesson, you should be able to describe some behaviors that help animals to survive and reproduce.

Male bower birds build stunning nests with colorful objects, such as berries and flowers, to attract females. This male also collected a brightly colored pen!

© Houghton Mifflin Harcourt Publishing Company • Image Credits: (bg) ©Dave Watts/Alamy Images

Engage Your Brain

1 Identify Unscramble the letters below to find four behaviors that help animals survive and reproduce. Write your words on the blank lines.

TANIGE _____

LGIENRNA _____

TNARPEIGN _____

TIMNAG _____

2 Describe Write your own caption to this photo.

_____

_____

_____

Active Reading

3 Synthesize Many English words have their roots in other languages. Use the Latin words below to make an educated guess about the meaning of the words *hibernation* and *estivation*.

Root word	Meaning
hibernus	of winter
aestas	of summer

Example sentence:
The snakes were <u>hibernating</u> to avoid the cold.

hibernation

_____

_____

Example sentence:
The frogs were <u>estivating</u> to avoid the heat.

estivation

_____

_____

Vocabulary Terms

- stimulus
- innate behavior
- learned behavior
- territory
- migration
- hibernation
- estivation
- social behavior

4 Apply As you learn the definition of each vocabulary term in this lesson, create your own definition or sketch to help you remember the meaning of the term.

How Stimulating!

What is behavior?

If your stomach grumbles when you wake up in the morning, you might go eat breakfast. Hunger is a **stimulus**, which is a type of information that causes a reaction or change in an organism. In this case, the response is a behavioral change. You go from lying in bed to looking for food. Behavior is the set of actions taken by an organism in response to stimuli.

Stimuli can be internal or external. An internal stimulus, such as feeling sick or feverish, comes from within an animal's body. When you get sick, your behavior can change. For example, you may choose to rest or no longer eat whatever caused your sickness.

An external stimulus comes from outside the body. These stimuli give animals information about their surroundings. If a rabbit hears a fox hunting nearby, the rabbit might run away. The sound of a fox is an external stimulus.

Visualize It!

6 Infer Consider the colorful individual below. How might color vision help mantis shrimp survive?

_____

_____

_____

_____

Animal sensory systems detect external stimuli. Mantis shrimp eyes distinguish more colors than human eyes can detect.

© Houghton Mifflin Harcourt Publishing Company • Image Credits: ©Imagebroker/Alamy Images

How does behavior develop?

Animals are born knowing how to perform certain behaviors. A calf knows how to nurse as soon as it is born. All calves perform this behavior when they are born. However, some behaviors occur only if they are learned during an animal's life. A pet dog can learn to sit in response to its owner's command. But dogs will sit on command only if they are trained.

Some Behaviors Are Innate

Behavior that develops without depending on learning or experience is **innate behavior**. Animals perform an innate behavior completely the first time they try it. For example, a person's first yawn is just like every other time he or she yawns. A mother goose retrieves any eggs that roll from her nest by rolling them back to the nest with her bill. She does not need another goose to show her how to act this way. This behavior is known by the goose without any learning or previous experience.

Newborn whales have the innate ability to swim. They know how to swim without learning.

Some Behaviors Are Learned

A behavior that develops through experience or from observing the actions of other animals is a **learned behavior**. Many animals learn through experience which places are most likely to have food available. Some birds learn their songs by listening to other individuals. Young dolphins can learn how to hunt by watching adults. Some dolphins learn to push sponges along the ocean floor to stir up food, but not all dolphins behave this way.

Lyrebirds learn their songs by imitating sounds in the environment. They even imitate sounds such as cameras and chainsaws!

8 Identify Which human behaviors are innate, and which are learned? List some examples below.

Innate	Learned
laughing	playing the piano

Survival Skills

What behaviors help animals survive?

In order to survive, animals need to be able to avoid danger. They must also be able to find food and water. Animals have a variety of behaviors to stay safe and to find and defend food, water, shelter, and mates. Behaviors used to find food are called *foraging* behaviors.

Finding Food

All animals need food to survive. Animals that eat plants must find and identify the right plants. Getting enough food can take a lot of time. Giant pandas need to spend up to 14 hours a day eating bamboo. Squirrels bury food to store it for eating at a later time when food is hard to find.

Predators are animals that eat other individuals, called prey. Predators have different strategies to capture their prey. Some use speed and strength to catch prey. But others use lures, tools, or traps. The alligator snapping turtle has a pink, worm-like lure in its mouth. It waits with its mouth open to lure fish to the "worm." When a fish comes close, the turtle snaps it up.

Spiders build webs to trap their prey. When an insect hits the web, the spider moves quickly to find its meal.

9 Identify What are two strategies that predators use to capture prey?

_____

_____

Marking Territories

Many animals must protect mates, offspring, or resources such as food. To do this, some animals mark a **territory**, an area occupied by a group or an individual. Marking a territory signals others of the same species not to enter the area. Birds mark territories by singing. Mammals rub the bark from trees or release chemical signals.

Cheetahs have a territorial imperative, which means they need to mark a territory. They do so by leaving a scent on trees.

Defending Resources

Many animals must defend their food, mates, and offspring from competition. Sometimes animals will fight to defend their resources. But usually they have behaviors that help them avoid fighting. Fighting is dangerous for both the winners and the losers. A common strategy to avoid fighting is trying to look bigger. Looking bigger can convince the competition to give up.

Many male **Anolis** lizards puff out colorful throat flaps, called dewlaps, to threaten other males.

Avoiding Danger

Avoiding danger is an important part of survival. Some animals are fast and can run away to escape predators. The European hare can run as fast as 72 kilometers per hour! A few animals can change color to blend in to the environment and avoid predators. Octopi and cuttlefish can change their color to quickly match a background. Some animals avoid predators by releasing toxic chemicals. Skunks and stinkbugs release a chemical that drives predators away. Some animals can trick predators by appearing too big to eat. Pufferfish can avoid predation by puffing up their bodies when threatened.

Can you see the octopus in this photograph? It uses camouflage to avoid predators.

Active Reading 10 **Identify** What are three behaviors that animals use to avoid danger?

_____

_____

_____

Octopi can squirt ink to confuse predators. This allows them to escape unharmed.

Inquiry

11 **Infer** Not many animals can change color to camouflage themselves against a background. What is another behavior that animals could use to be camouflaged against a background?

_____

_____

_____

© Houghton Mifflin Harcourt Publishing Company • Image Credits: (t) ©Karl Shone/Dorling Kindersley/Getty Images; (c) ©Stockbyte/Getty Images; (bl) ©Eiichi Kurasawa/Photo Researchers, Inc.

A Success Story

What behaviors help animals reproduce successfully?

Animals have behaviors that help them reproduce successfully. Courtship behaviors help individuals find a mate. Parenting behaviors help animals raise healthy young. Many strange and beautiful animal behaviors relate to courtship and parenting.

Courtship

Many of the bright colors and complex calls of animals are used to help find a mate. Males use a variety of behaviors to try attracting females. Some birds and fish build eye-catching nests. Some insects bring gifts of food to convince females to mate. Many males have displays that stand out and get a female's attention. Adelie penguins call loudly, lift their head, and flap their flippers. Male jumping spiders perform fast dances that attract nearby females. Some females participate in courtship behaviors, too. Male and female sandhill cranes dance together by running, jumping, and flapping their wings.

Male and female fireflies "flash" each other to signal that they are ready to mate.

Parenting

Parents can help their young survive in many ways. Young killer whales learn to hunt by watching the adults. Many kinds of bird parents bring food to babies that are too weak to leave the nest. Mother killdeer birds behave as though their wing is broken to lure predators away from the nest.

Parents may help their young for just a short time or for quite a while. Some animals parent only long enough to lay eggs in a protected place. Mother chimpanzees parent their daughters for many years. Not all animals exhibit parenting behaviors.

Many birds hatch as helpless young that depend upon their parents to feed them.

Visualize It!

12 Apply How do you think the young in the photo let the parents know that they need food?

_____

_____

_____

What behaviors help animals survive seasonal change?

Seasonal changes can make survival difficult. A change in temperature can make it hard to find food or raise young. Animals have a few strategies to survive seasonal changes. Both daily cycles, or *circadian rhythms* (ser•KAY•dee•uhn RITH•uhmz), and seasonal cycles of behavior are controlled by biological clocks. A *biological clock* is an internal control of an animal's natural cycles.

Moving to Good Conditions

When seasonal weather changes make it hard to survive, some animals migrate. **Migration** is a seasonal movement from one place to another. Monarch butterflies cannot survive cold, northern winters. So they fly south when the weather cools. In the spring, they mate and fly north again. Many kinds of invertebrates, fish, amphibians, reptiles, birds, and mammals migrate. Animals that migrate depend on a biological clock to signal when to move.

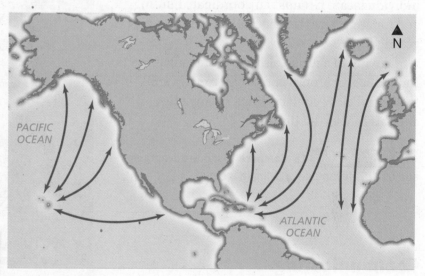

Waiting for Good Conditions

Animals that don't migrate can become inactive until seasonal conditions improve. **Hibernation** is a period of inactivity and decreased body temperature that some animals experience in winter. **Estivation** is a period of inactivity experienced during hot and dry summers. A biological clock signals when to begin and end these seasonal behaviors.

14 Infer What do people do to make it through seasonal conditions such as cold winters or hot summers?

_____

_____

_____

Humpback whales move between cold, northern waters where they feed and warm, southern waters where they give birth.

A hibernating dormouse's temperature can drop to just above the environmental temperature.

Social Structure

What are some social animal behaviors?

Animals have many social behaviors, such as those to communicate, hunt, and reproduce. **Social behavior** is the set of interactions that occur among animals of the same species.

Living in Groups

Many animals live in groups. A group of lions is called a *pride.* A group of geese is called a *gaggle.* Living in a group has some advantages. A group can spot a predator more quickly than an individual can. Groups can coordinate hunting and foraging, so everyone has a better chance of getting food.

   Living in a group also has disadvantages. Individuals in groups compete for mates and food. And close contact with so many other animals can spread disease.

Active Reading 15 **Compare** List one advantage and one disadvantage of living in a group.

_____

_____

Communicating

Animals communicate to influence the behavior of others. Many signals relate to danger, food, and mating. Many male birds perform colorful dance displays to catch a female's eye. Bees signal where to find food with both sound and scent in a "waggle dance."

   Some animals communicate by sound, sight, or touch. Elephants make sounds that are too low for humans to hear. Some animals communicate with chemicals. *Pheromones* (FEHR•uh•mohnz) are chemicals released by one animal that affect the behavior of others. Moths release pheromones to attract a mate. Ants leave pheromone paths to help others find food.

Meerkats make many kinds of calls to communicate with other meerkats in their large social groups.

16 **Infer** Meerkats make different alarm calls for different types of predators. How do you think this could help meerkats survive?

_____

_____

_____

_____

Forming a "Pecking Order"

People who own chickens can easily recognize a pecking order. One bird is the most dominant and has first access to food. Another is the bottom bird who lets all of the other birds get food before it has a turn. Groups that have clearly dominant individuals have a *social hierarchy* (SOH•shuhl HY•uh•rar•kee). Wolves also have a social hierarchy. The dominant male and female pair is called the alpha pair. All of the other wolves in the pack will follow the alpha pair's lead. The alpha pair decides when to hunt and when to rest. In a social hierarchy, individuals can sometimes fight to change their status.

When dominant baboons approach, less dominant animals move away.

Living Within a Set Structure

Some animals have a social structure that is determined from birth. In a honeybee colony, one individual is the queen. She is the only bee that lays eggs, and her position lasts her entire life. All bees in the colony come from her eggs, so all the bees are closely related. The queen's offspring include workers that clean, feed larvae, build, and find food. The workers do each job at a different stage of life. Young workers clean the hive. Older workers forage for food that they share. A bee colony is an example of a set social structure. Several insects that are very closely related have this type of social organization.

17 Compare How are social hierarchies different from set social structures?

_____

_____

_____

_____

_____

_____

_____

These weaver ants are workers that are building a safe nest for the colony.

Visual Summary

To complete this summary, write the answers to the questions on the lines. Then, use the key below to check your answers. You can use this page to review the main concepts of the lesson.

Behavior is a response to internal or external stimuli.

18 What are learned and innate behaviors?

_____

_____

_____

Social behavior is the set of interactions between individuals of one species.

20 What are three examples of social behaviors in animals?

_____

_____

_____

Animal Behavior

Many behaviors help animals survive and reproduce successfully.

19 What is a biological clock?

_____

_____

_____

Answers: 18 innate: do not depend on experience; learned: depend on experience; 19 the internal control of an animal's natural cycles; 20 living in groups, communication, and reproduction

21 Synthesize Describe an animal behavior that you have seen recently where you live or on TV. Identify the stimulus that caused the behavioral response, and explain how that behavior might help the animal survive.

Lesson Review

Vocabulary

Draw a line to connect the following terms to their definitions.

1 territory

2 innate

3 estivation

A a behavior that does not depend on experience

B a period of inactivity that occurs during hot and dry conditions

C an area occupied by one or more animals that do not allow other members of the species to enter

Key Concepts

4 Identify What is the difference between internal stimuli and external stimuli?

_____

_____

_____

5 Describe Choose one animal and describe how it marks its territory.

_____

_____

_____

6 Explain How do animals use pheromones?

_____

_____

_____

7 Compare What are the advantages and disadvantages of living in a group?

_____

_____

_____

Critical Thinking

Use this map to answer the following questions.

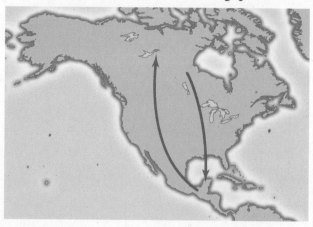

8 Analyze Which of the following behaviors could be represented by the arrows: migration, hibernation, or estivation?

_____

_____

9 Infer How would the birds traveling along this path know when to move from place to place?

_____

_____

_____

10 Relate What behaviors do humans use to find food, parent their offspring, and court each other?

_____

_____

_____

_____

_____

11 Apply Explain how looking bigger by spreading its wings might help a bird avoid predation.

_____

_____

_____

_____

_____

My Notes

7 The picture below shows a virus.

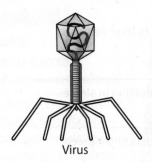

Virus

Which of the following is a task the host cell has during the replication of viruses?

A The host cell destroys the virus.

B The host cell replicates the virus's genetic material.

C The host cell is destroyed and viral replication stops.

D The host cell's proteins block the replication of the viral proteins.

8 Which of the following is true of protists?

A Protists reproduce only by asexual reproduction.

B Some protists can photosynthesize.

C Protists cannot move on their own.

D Protists are prokaryotic.

9 Fungi that exist mostly in a unicellular state and reproduce by budding are called what?

A molds

B hyphae

C spores

D yeasts

10 Where would you expect to see a plant that does not have a vascular system?

A in a botanical museum, because they are all extinct

B deeply rooted in a forest with a trunk that reaches 20 meters or more

C low and close to the ground

D climbing high while circling the branches of another plant

11 Which of the following is a plant structure that is involved in asexual reproduction?

A stigma   **C** pistil

B stamen   **D** tuber

12 The diagram below shows a cycle of energy flowing between living organisms.

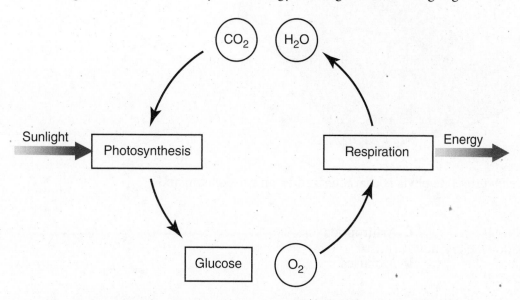

Which of the following could the two sides of the diagram represent?

A The left side represents a producer, and the right side represents a consumer.

B The left side represents a consumer, and the right side represents a producer.

C The left side represents an animal that eats plants, and the right side represents a plant.

D The left side represents energy created, and the right side represents energy destroyed.

13 Which of the following is true of all animals?

A They are producers.

B They are multicellular.

C They reproduce asexually.

D They are unicellular.

14 The fossil below shows a well-preserved invertebrate with an exoskeleton and jointed appendages.

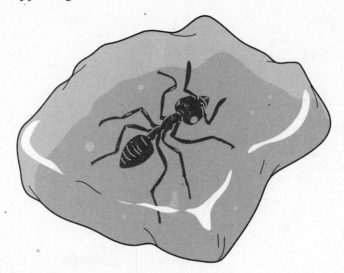

Which of these invertebrate phyla is characterized by an exoskeleton and jointed legs?

A Cnidaria

C Arthropoda

B Ctenophora

D Mollusca

15 Which of the following phrases describes the cycle of activity that an animal has during any 24-hour period?

A the animal's hibernation period

B the animal's estivation period

C the animal's biological clock

D the animal's circadian rhythm

16 Which of the following describes an innate animal behavior?

A a pet dog shaking hands on its owner's command

B Monarch butterflies migrating southward

C squirrels in a park approaching people for food

D a horse being ridden through an obstacle course

17 The diagram below shows the relationships among some members of the phylum Chordata.

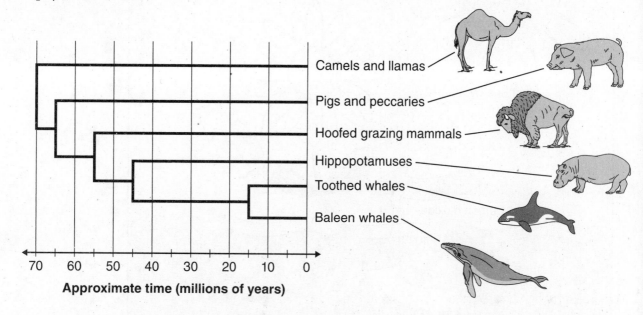

Camels and llamas

Pigs and peccaries

Hoofed grazing mammals

Hippopotamuses

Toothed whales

Baleen whales

Approximate time (millions of years)

70 60 50 40 30 20 10 0

Which trait is shared by all members of the phylum Chordata?

A a notochord   **C** gills

B hollow bones   **D** radial symmetry

Critical Thinking

Answer the following questions in the space provided.

18 Describe how flowering plants reproduce through sexual reproduction.

_____

_____

_____

_____

19 Many plants grow in the spring and summer and become dormant during the fall and winter. Explain what triggers dormancy in a plant, and explain the benefits of winter dormancy for those plants.

_____

_____

_____

_____

_____

20 The diagram below shows the process in which plants use energy from the sun.

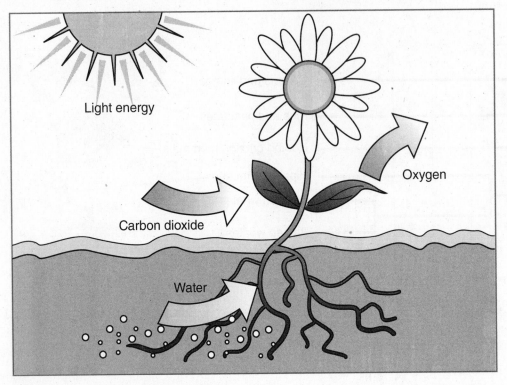

What is this process called? _____

In which plant organelle does this process occur? _____

How does the plant store the energy it gets from the sun?

_____

_____

Is a plant a producer, consumer, or decomposer? _____

Connect ESSENTIAL QUESTIONS
Lessons 3, 5, and 6

Answer the following question in the space provided.

21 Explain how the vascular systems of plants in the rainforests might have affected animal behavior and the diversity of life in the rainforests.

_____

_____

_____

_____

_____

Look It Up!

References

Mineral Properties

Here are five steps to take in mineral identification:

1 Determine the color of the mineral. Is it light-colored, dark-colored, or a specific color?

2 Determine the luster of the mineral. Is it metallic or non-metallic?

3 Determine the color of any powder left by its streak.

4 Determine the hardness of your mineral. Is it soft, hard, or very hard? Using a glass plate, see if the mineral scratches it.

5 Determine whether your sample has cleavage or any special properties.

TERMS TO KNOW	DEFINITION
adamantine	a non-metallic luster like that of a diamond
cleavage	how a mineral breaks when subject to stress on a particular plane
luster	the state or quality of shining by reflecting light
streak	the color of a mineral when it is powdered
submetallic	between metallic and nonmetallic in luster
vitreous	glass-like type of luster

Silicate Minerals					
Mineral	**Color**	**Luster**	**Streak**	**Hardness**	**Cleavage and Special Properties**
Beryl	deep green, pink, white, bluish green, or yellow	vitreous	white	7.5–8	1 cleavage direction; some varieties fluoresce in ultraviolet light
Chlorite	green	vitreous to pearly	pale green	2–2.5	1 cleavage direction
Garnet	green, red, brown, black	vitreous	white	6.5–7.5	no cleavage
Hornblende	dark green, brown, or black	vitreous	none	5–6	2 cleavage directions
Muscovite	colorless, silvery white, or brown	vitreous or pearly	white	2–2.5	1 cleavage direction
Olivine	olive green, yellow	vitreous	white or none	6.5–7	no cleavage
Orthoclase	colorless, white, pink, or other colors	vitreous	white or none	6	2 cleavage directions
Plagioclase	colorless, white, yellow, pink, green	vitreous	white	6	2 cleavage directions
Quartz	colorless or white; any color when not pure	vitreous or waxy	white or none	7	no cleavage

Nonsilicate Minerals					
Mineral	**Color**	**Luster**	**Streak**	**Hardness**	**Cleavage and Special Properties**
Native Elements					
Copper	copper-red	metallic	copper-red	2.5–3	no cleavage
Diamond	pale yellow or colorless	adamantine	none	10	4 cleavage directions
Graphite	black to gray	submetallic	black	1–2	1 cleavage direction
Carbonates					
Aragonite	colorless, white, or pale yellow	vitreous	white	3.5–4	2 cleavage directions; reacts with hydrochloric acid
Calcite	colorless or white to tan	vitreous	white	3	3 cleavage directions; reacts with weak acid; double refraction
Halides					
Fluorite	light green, yellow, purple, bluish green, or other colors	vitreous	none	4	4 cleavage directions; some varieties fluoresce
Halite	white	vitreous	white	2.0–2.5	3 cleavage directions
Oxides					
Hematite	reddish brown to black	metallic to earthy	dark red to red-brown	5.6–6.5	no cleavage; magnetic when heated
Magnetite	iron-black	metallic	black	5.5–6.5	no cleavage; magnetic
Sulfates					
Anhydrite	colorless, bluish, or violet	vitreous to pearly	white	3–3.5	3 cleavage directions
Gypsum	white, pink, gray, or colorless	vitreous, pearly, or silky	white	2.0	3 cleavage directions
Sulfides					
Galena	lead-gray	metallic	lead-gray to black	2.5–2.8	3 cleavage directions
Pyrite	brassy yellow	metallic	greenish, brownish, or black	6–6.5	no cleavage

References

Geologic Time Scale

Geologists developed the geologic time scale to represent the 4.6 billion years of Earth's history that have passed since Earth formed. This scale divides Earth's history into blocks of time. The boundaries between these time intervals (shown in millions of years ago or mya in the table below), represent major changes in Earth's history. Some boundaries are defined by mass extinctions, major changes in Earth's surface, and/or major changes in Earth's climate.

The four major divisions that encompass the history of life on Earth are Precambrian time, the Paleozoic era, the Mesozoic era, and the Cenozoic era. The largest divisions are eons. **Precambrian time** is made up of the first three eons, over 4 billion years of Earth's history.

The **Paleozoic era** lasted from 542 mya to 251 mya. All major plant groups, except flowering plants, appeared during this era. By the end of the era, reptiles, winged insects, and fishes had also appeared. The largest known mass extinction occurred at the end of this era.

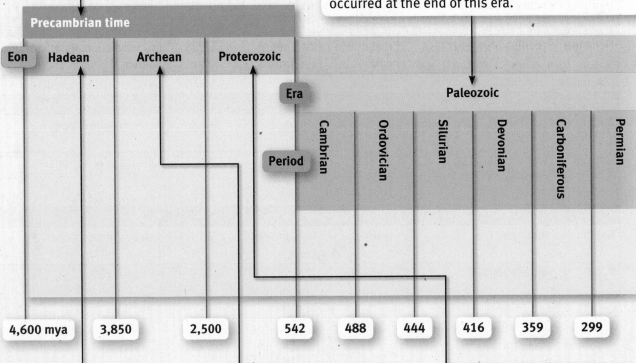

The **Hadean eon** lasted from about 4.6 billion years ago (bya) to 3.85 bya. It is described based on evidence from meterorites and rocks from the moon.

The **Archean eon** lasted from 3.85 bya to 2.5 bya. The earliest rocks from Earth that have been found and dated formed at the start of this eon.

The **Proterozoic eon** lasted from 2.5 bya to 542 mya. The first organisms, which were single-celled organisms, appeared during this eon. These organisms produced so much oxygen that they changed Earth's oceans and Earth's atmosphere.

Divisions of Time

The divisions of time shown here represent major changes in Earth's surface and when life developed and changed significantly on Earth. As new evidence is found, the boundaries of these divisions may shift. The Phanerozoic eon is divided into three eras. The beginning of each of these eras represents a change in the types of organisms that dominated Earth. And, each era is commonly characterized by the types of organisms that dominated the era. These eras are divided into periods, and periods are divided into epochs.

The **Mesozoic era** lasted from 251 mya to 65.5 mya. During this era, many kinds of dinosaurs dominated land, and giant lizards swam in the ocean. The first birds, mammals, and flowering plants also appeared during this time. About two-thirds of all land species went extinct at the end of this era.

The **Phanerozoic eon** began 542 mya. We live in this eon.

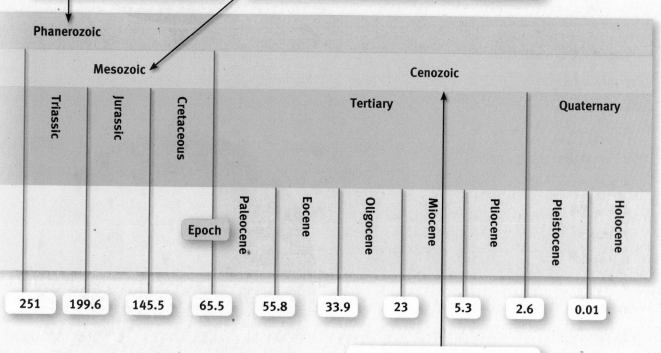

The **Cenozoic era** began 65.5 mya and continues today. Mammals dominate this era. During the Mesozoic era, mammals were small in size but grew much larger during the Cenozoic era. Primates, including humans, appeared during this era.

Star Charts for the Northern Hemisphere

A star chart is a map of the stars in the night sky. It shows the names and positions of constellations and major stars. Star charts can be used to identify constellations and even to orient yourself using Polaris, the North Star.

Because Earth moves through space, different constellations are visible at different times of the year. The star charts on these pages show the constellations visible during each season in the Northern Hemisphere.

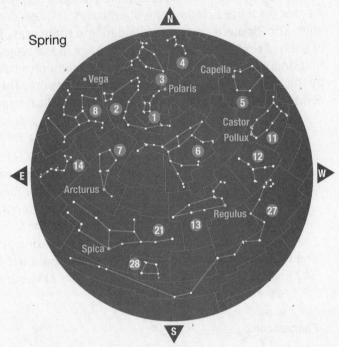

Spring

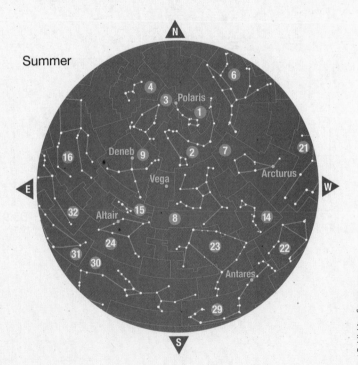

Summer

Constellations

1 Ursa Minor

2 Draco

3 Cepheus

4 Cassiopeia

5 Auriga

6 Ursa Major

7 Boötes

8 Hercules

9 Cygnus

10 Perseus

11 Gemini

12 Cancer

13 Leo

14 Serpens

15 Sagitta

16 Pegasus

17 Pisces

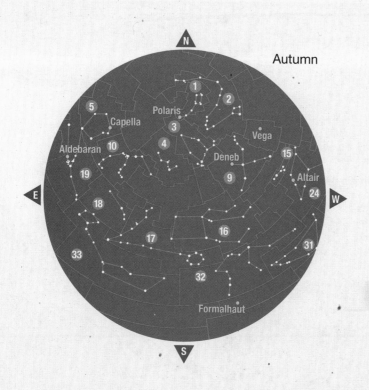

Autumn

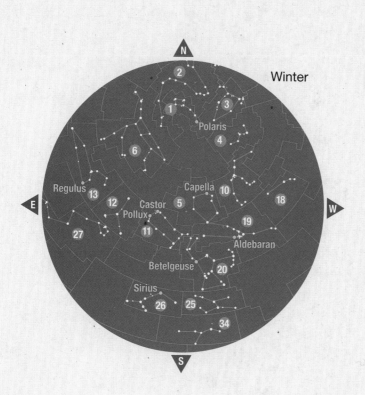

Winter

Constellations

18 Aries

19 Taurus

20 Orion

21 Virgo

22 Libra

23 Ophiuchus

24 Aquila

25 Lepus

26 Canis Major

27 Hydra

28 Corvus

29 Scorpius

30 Sagittarius

31 Capricornus

32 Aquarius

33 Cetus

34 Columba

World Map

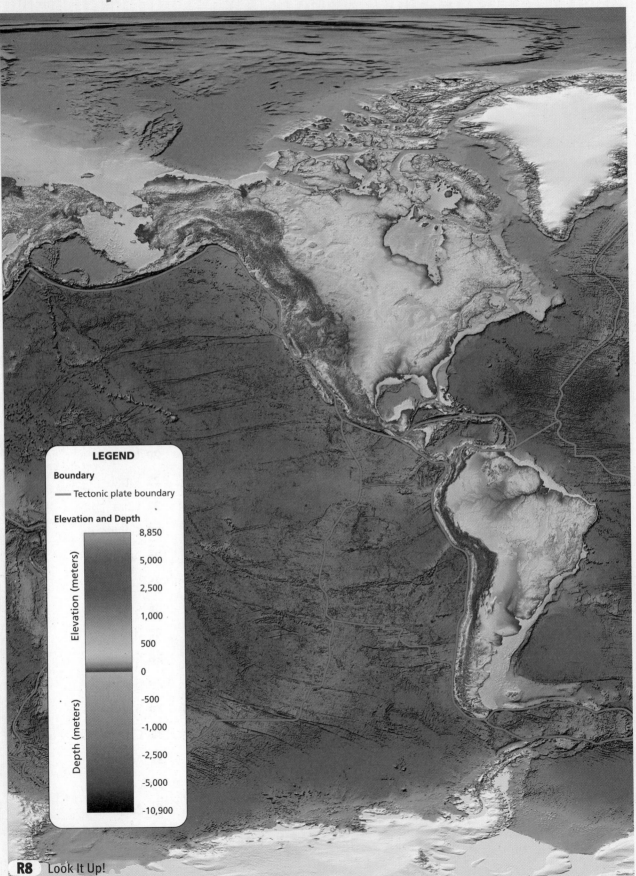

LEGEND

Boundary

—— Tectonic plate boundary

Elevation and Depth

Elevation (meters)

- 8,850
- 5,000
- 2,500
- 1,000
- 500
- 0

Depth (meters)

- -500
- -1,000
- -2,500
- -5,000
- -10,900

References

Classification of Living Things

Domains and Kingdoms

All organisms belong to one of three domains: Domain Archaea, Domain Bacteria, or Domain Eukarya. Some of the groups within these domains are shown below. (Remember that genus names are italicized.)

Domain Archaea

The organisms in this domain are single-celled prokaryotes, many of which live in extreme environments.

Archaea		
Group	Example	Characteristics
Methanogens	*Methanococcus*	produce methane gas; can't live in oxygen
Thermophiles	*Sulpholobus*	require sulphur; can't live in oxygen
Halophiles	*Halococcus*	live in very salty environments; most can live in oxygen

Domain Bacteria

Organisms in this domain are single-celled prokaryotes and are found in almost every environment on Earth.

Bacteria		
Group	Example	Characteristics
Bacilli	*Escherichia*	rod shaped; some bacilli fix nitrogen; some cause disease
Cocci	*Streptococcus*	spherical shaped; some cause disease; can form spores
Spirilla	*Treponema*	spiral shaped; cause diseases such as syphilis and Lyme disease

Domain Eukarya

Organisms in this domain are single-celled or multicellular eukaryotes.

Kingdom Protista Many protists resemble fungi, plants, or animals, but are smaller and simpler in structure. Most are single celled.

Protists		
Group	Example	Characteristics
Sarcodines	*Amoeba*	radiolarians; single-celled consumers
Ciliates	*Paramecium*	single-celled consumers
Flagellates	*Trypanosoma*	single-celled parasites
Sporozoans	*Plasmodium*	single-celled parasites
Euglenas	*Euglena*	single celled; photosynthesize
Diatoms	*Pinnularia*	most are single celled; photosynthesize
Dinoflagellates	*Gymnodinium*	single celled; some photosynthesize
Algae	*Volvox*	single celled or multicellular; photosynthesize
Slime molds	*Physarum*	single celled or multicellular; consumers or decomposers
Water molds	powdery mildew	single celled or multicellular; parasites or decomposers

Kingdom Fungi Most fungi are multicellular. Their cells have thick cell walls. Fungi absorb food from their environment.

Fungi		
Group	**Examples**	**Characteristics**
Threadlike fungi	bread mold	spherical; decomposers
Sac fungi	yeast; morels	saclike; parasites and decomposers
Club fungi	mushrooms; rusts; smuts	club shaped; parasites and decomposers
Lichens	British soldier	a partnership between a fungus and an alga

Kingdom Plantae Plants are multicellular and have cell walls made of cellulose. Plants make their own food through photosynthesis. Plants are classified into divisions instead of phyla.

Plants		
Group	**Examples**	**Characteristics**
Bryophytes	mosses; liverworts	no vascular tissue; reproduce by spores
Club mosses	*Lycopodium;* ground pine	grow in wooded areas; reproduce by spores
Horsetails	rushes	grow in wetland areas; reproduce by spores
Ferns	spleenworts; sensitive fern	large leaves called fronds; reproduce by spores
Conifers	pines; spruces; firs	needlelike leaves; reproduce by seeds made in cones
Cycads	*Zamia*	slow growing; reproduce by seeds made in large cones
Gnetophytes	*Welwitschia*	only three living families; reproduce by seeds
Ginkgoes	*Ginkgo*	only one living species; reproduce by seeds
Angiosperms	all flowering plants	reproduce by seeds made in flowers; fruit

Kingdom Animalia Animals are multicellular. Their cells do not have cell walls. Most animals have specialized tissues and complex organ systems. Animals get food by eating other organisms.

Animals		
Group	**Examples**	**Characteristics**
Sponges	glass sponges	no symmetry or specialized tissues; aquatic
Cnidarians	jellyfish; coral	radial symmetry; aquatic
Flatworms	planaria; tapeworms; flukes	bilateral symmetry; organ systems
Roundworms	*Trichina;* hookworms	bilateral symmetry; organ systems
Annelids	earthworms; leeches	bilateral symmetry; organ systems
Mollusks	snails; octopuses	bilateral symmetry; organ systems
Echinoderms	sea stars; sand dollars	radial symmetry; organ systems
Arthropods	insects; spiders; lobsters	bilateral symmetry; organ systems
Chordates	fish; amphibians; reptiles; birds; mammals	bilateral symmetry; complex organ systems

References

Periodic Table of the Elements

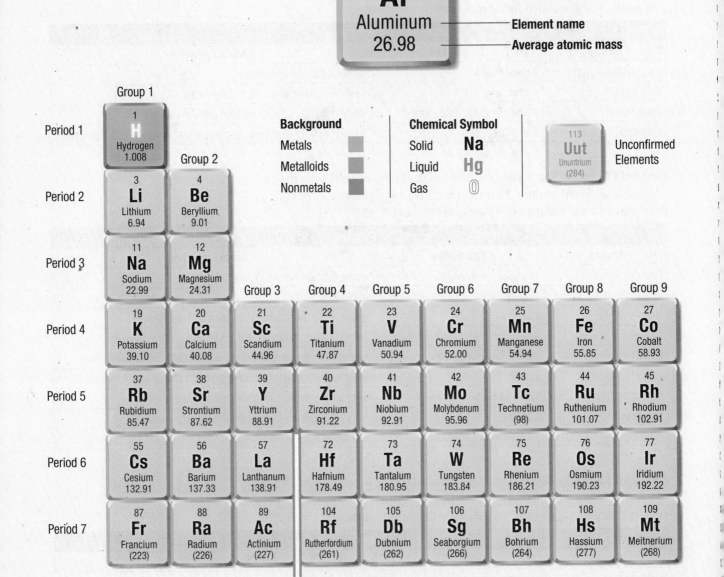

	13
	Al
	Aluminum
	26.98

- Atomic number
- Chemical symbol
- Element name
- Average atomic mass

Background
- Metals
- Metalloids
- Nonmetals

Chemical Symbol
- Solid **Na**
- Liquid **Hg**
- Gas ⓞ

113 **Uut** Ununtrium (284) — Unconfirmed Elements

Group 1

| Period 1 | 1 **H** Hydrogen 1.008 |

Group 2

| Period 2 | 3 **Li** Lithium 6.94 | 4 **Be** Beryllium 9.01 |

| Period 3 | 11 **Na** Sodium 22.99 | 12 **Mg** Magnesium 24.31 |

			Group 3	Group 4	Group 5	Group 6	Group 7	Group 8	Group 9
Period 4	19 **K** Potassium 39.10	20 **Ca** Calcium 40.08	21 **Sc** Scandium 44.96	22 **Ti** Titanium 47.87	23 **V** Vanadium 50.94	24 **Cr** Chromium 52.00	25 **Mn** Manganese 54.94	26 **Fe** Iron 55.85	27 **Co** Cobalt 58.93
Period 5	37 **Rb** Rubidium 85.47	38 **Sr** Strontium 87.62	39 **Y** Yttrium 88.91	40 **Zr** Zirconium 91.22	41 **Nb** Niobium 92.91	42 **Mo** Molybdenum 95.96	43 **Tc** Technetium (98)	44 **Ru** Ruthenium 101.07	45 **Rh** Rhodium 102.91
Period 6	55 **Cs** Cesium 132.91	56 **Ba** Barium 137.33	57 **La** Lanthanum 138.91	72 **Hf** Hafnium 178.49	73 **Ta** Tantalum 180.95	74 **W** Tungsten 183.84	75 **Re** Rhenium 186.21	76 **Os** Osmium 190.23	77 **Ir** Iridium 192.22
Period 7	87 **Fr** Francium (223)	88 **Ra** Radium (226)	89 **Ac** Actinium (227)	104 **Rf** Rutherfordium (261)	105 **Db** Dubnium (262)	106 **Sg** Seaborgium (266)	107 **Bh** Bohrium (264)	108 **Hs** Hassium (277)	109 **Mt** Meitnerium (268)

Lanthanides

58 **Ce** Cerium 140.12	59 **Pr** Praseodymium 140.91	60 **Nd** Neodymium 144.24	61 **Pm** Promethium (145)	62 **Sm** Samarium 150.36

Actinides

90 **Th** Thorium 232.04	91 **Pa** Protactinium 231.04	92 **U** Uranium 238.03	93 **Np** Neptunium (237)	94 **Pu** Plutonium (244)

The International Union of Pure and Applied Chemistry (IUPAC) has determined that, because of isotopic variance, the average atomic mass is best represented by a range of values for each of the following elements: hydrogen, lithium, boron, carbon, nitrogen, oxygen, silicon, sulfur, chlorine, and thallium. However, the values in this table are appropriate for everyday calculations.

			Group 18
			2 **He** Helium 4.003

Group 13	Group 14	Group 15	Group 16	Group 17	
5 **B** Boron 10.81	6 **C** Carbon 12.01	7 **N** Nitrogen 14.01	8 **O** Oxygen 16.00	9 **F** Fluorine 19.00	10 **Ne** Neon 20.18
13 **Al** Aluminum 26.98	14 **Si** Silicon 28.09	15 **P** Phosphorus 30.97	16 **S** Sulfur 32.06	17 **Cl** Chlorine 35.45	18 **Ar** Argon 39.95

Group 10	Group 11	Group 12					
28 **Ni** Nickel 58.69	29 **Cu** Copper 63.55	30 **Zn** Zinc 65.38	31 **Ga** Gallium 69.72	32 **Ge** Germanium 72.63	33 **As** Arsenic 74.92	34 **Se** Selenium 78.96	35 **Br** Bromine 79.90	36 **Kr** Krypton 83.80
46 **Pd** Palladium 106.42	47 **Ag** Silver 107.87	48 **Cd** Cadmium 112.41	49 **In** Indium 114.82	50 **Sn** Tin 118.71	51 **Sb** Antimony 121.76	52 **Te** Tellurium 127.60	53 **I** Iodine 126.90	54 **Xe** Xenon 131.29
78 **Pt** Platinum 195.08	79 **Au** Gold 196.97	80 **Hg** Mercury 200.59	81 **Tl** Thallium 204.38	82 **Pb** Lead 207.2	83 **Bi** Bismuth 208.98	84 **Po** Polonium (209)	85 **At** Astatine (210)	86 **Rn** Radon (222)
110 **Ds** Darmstadtium (271)	111 **Rg** Roentgenium (272)	112 **Cn** Copernicium (285)	113 **Uut** Ununtrium (284)	114 **Uuq** Ununquadium (289)	115 **Uup** Ununpentium (288)	116 **Uuh** Ununhexium (292)	117 **Uus** Ununseptium (294)	118 **Uuo** Ununoctium (294)

63 **Eu** Europium 151.96	64 **Gd** Gadolinium 157.25	65 **Tb** Terbium 158.93	66 **Dy** Dysprosium 162.50	67 **Ho** Holmium 164.93	68 **Er** Erbium 167.26	69 **Tm** Thulium 168.93	70 **Yb** Ytterbium 173.05	71 **Lu** Lutetium 174.97
95 **Am** Americium (243)	96 **Cm** Curium (247)	97 **Bk** Berkelium (247)	98 **Cf** Californium (251)	99 **Es** Einsteinium (252)	100 **Fm** Fermium (257)	101 **Md** Mendelevium (258)	102 **No** Nobelium (259)	103 **Lr** Lawrencium (262)

References

Physical Science Refresher

Atoms and Elements

Every object in the universe is made of matter. **Matter** is anything that takes up space and has mass. All matter is made of atoms. An **atom** is the smallest particle into which an element can be divided and still be the same element. An **element**, in turn, is a substance that cannot be broken down into simpler substances by chemical means. Each element consists of only one kind of atom. An element may be made of many atoms, but they are all the same kind of atom.

Atomic Structure

Atoms are made of smaller particles called **electrons**, **protons**, and **neutrons**. Electrons have a negative electric charge, protons have a positive charge, and neutrons have no electric charge. Together, protons and neutrons form the **nucleus**, or small dense center, of an atom. Because protons are positively charged and neutrons are neutral, the nucleus has a positive charge. Electrons move within an area around the nucleus called the **electron cloud**. Electrons move so quickly that scientists cannot determine their exact speeds and positions at the same time.

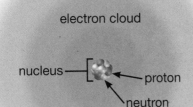

electron cloud

nucleus — proton

neutron

Atomic Number

To help distinguish one element from another, scientists use the atomic numbers of atoms. The **atomic number** is the number of protons in the nucleus of an atom. The atoms of a certain element always have the same number of protons.

When atoms have an equal number of protons and electrons, they are uncharged, or electrically neutral. The atomic number equals the number of electrons in an uncharged atom. The number of neutrons, however, can vary for a given element. Atoms of the same element that have different numbers of neutrons are called **isotopes**.

Periodic Table of the Elements

In the periodic table, each element in the table is in a separate box. And the elements are arranged from left to right in order of increasing atomic number. That is, an uncharged atom of each element has one more electron and one more proton than an uncharged atom of the element to its left. Each horizontal row of the table is called a **period**. Changes in chemical properties of elements across a period correspond to changes in the electron arrangements of their atoms.

Each vertical column of the table is known as a **group.** A group lists elements with similar physical and chemical properties. For this reason, a group is also sometimes called a family. The elements in a group have similar properties because their atoms have the same number of electrons in their outer energy level. For example, the elements helium, neon, argon, krypton, xenon, and radon all have similar properties and are known as the noble gases.

Molecules and Compounds

When two or more elements join chemically, they form a **compound**. A compound is a new substance with properties different from those of the elements that compose it. For example, water, H_2O, is a compound formed when hydrogen (H) and oxygen (O) combine. The smallest complete unit of a compound that has the properties of that compound is called a **molecule**. A chemical formula indicates the elements in a compound. It also indicates the relative number of atoms of each element in the compound. The chemical formula for water is H_2O. So, each water molecule consists of two atoms of hydrogen and one atom of oxygen. The subscript number after the symbol for an element shows how many atoms of that element are in a single molecule of the compound.

Chemical Equations

A chemical reaction occurs when a chemical change takes place. A chemical equation describes a chemical reaction using chemical formulas. The equation indicates the substances that react and the substances that are produced. For example, when carbon and oxygen combine, they can form carbon dioxide, shown in the equation below: $C + O_2 \longrightarrow CO_2$

Acids, Bases, and pH

An **ion** is an atom or group of chemically bonded atoms that has an electric charge because it has lost or gained one or more electrons. When an acid, such as hydrochloric acid, HCl, is mixed with water, it separates into ions. An **acid** is a compound that produces hydrogen ions, H^+, in water. The hydrogen ions then combine with a water molecule to form a hydronium ion, H_3O^+. A **base**, on the other hand, is a substance that produces hydroxide ions, OH^-, in water.

To determine whether a solution is acidic or basic, scientists use pH. The **pH** of a solution is a measure of the hydronium ion concentration in a solution. The pH scale ranges from 0 to 14. Acids have a pH that is less than 7. The lower the number, the more acidic the solution. The middle point, pH = 7, is neutral, neither acidic nor basic. Bases have a pH that is greater than 7. The higher the number is, the more basic the solution.

The pH of Some Common Materials

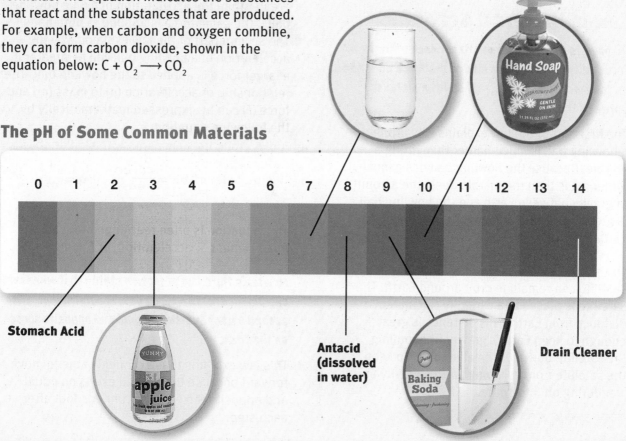

Stomach Acid

Antacid (dissolved in water)

Drain Cleaner

References

Physical Laws and Useful Equations

Law of Conservation of Mass

Mass cannot be created or destroyed during ordinary chemical or physical changes.

The total mass in a closed system is always the same no matter how many physical changes or chemical reactions occur.

Law of Conservation of Energy

Energy can be neither created nor destroyed.

The total amount of energy in a closed system is always the same. Energy can be changed from one form to another, but all of the different forms of energy in a system always add up to the same total amount of energy, no matter how many energy conversions occur.

Law of Universal Gravitation

All objects in the universe attract each other by a force called gravity. The size of the force depends on the masses of the objects and the distance between the objects.

The first part of the law explains why lifting a bowling ball is much harder than lifting a marble. Because the bowling ball has a much larger mass than the marble does, the amount of gravity between Earth and the bowling ball is greater than the amount of gravity between Earth and the marble.

The second part of the law explains why a satellite can remain in orbit around Earth. The satellite is placed at a carefully calculated distance from Earth. This distance is great enough to keep Earth's gravity from pulling the satellite down, yet small enough to keep the satellite from escaping Earth's gravity and wandering off into space.

Newton's Laws of Motion

Newton's first law of motion states that an object at rest remains at rest, and an object in motion remains in motion at constant speed and in a straight line unless acted on by an unbalanced force.

The first part of the law explains why a football will remain on a tee until it is kicked off or until a gust of wind blows it off. The second part of the law explains why a bike rider will continue moving forward after the bike comes to an abrupt stop. Gravity and the friction of the sidewalk will eventually stop the rider.

Newton's second law of motion states that the acceleration of an object depends on the mass of the object and the amount of force applied.

The first part of the law explains why the acceleration of a 4 kg bowling ball will be greater than the acceleration of a 6 kg bowling ball if the same force is applied to both balls. The second part of the law explains why the acceleration of a bowling ball will be greater if a larger force is applied to the bowling ball. The relationship of acceleration (a) to mass (m) and force (F) can be expressed mathematically by the following equation:

$$acceleration = \frac{force}{mass}, or\ a = \frac{F}{m}$$

This equation is often rearranged to read $force = mass \times acceleration$, or $F = m \times a$

Newton's third law of motion states that whenever one object exerts a force on a second object, the second object exerts an equal and opposite force on the first.

This law explains that a runner is able to move forward because the ground exerts an equal and opposite force on the runner's foot after each step.

Average speed

$$\text{average speed} = \frac{\text{total distance}}{\text{total time}}$$

Example:
A bicycle messenger traveled a distance of 136 km in 8 h. What was the messenger's average speed?

$$\frac{136 \text{ km}}{8 \text{ h}} = 17 \text{ km/h}$$

The messenger's average speed was **17 km/h**.

Average acceleration

$$\text{average acceleration} = \frac{\text{final velocity} - \text{starting velocity}}{\text{time it takes to change velocity}}$$

Example:
Calculate the average acceleration of an Olympic 100 m dash sprinter who reached a velocity of 20 m/s south at the finish line. The race was in a straight line and lasted 10 s.

$$\frac{20 \text{ m/s} - 0 \text{ m/s}}{10 \text{ s}} = 2 \text{ m/s/s}$$

The sprinter's average acceleration was **2 m/s/s south**.

Net force
Forces in the Same Direction

When forces are in the same direction, add the forces together to determine the net force.

Example:
Calculate the net force on a stalled car that is being pushed by two people. One person is pushing with a force of 13 N northwest, and the other person is pushing with a force of 8 N in the same direction.

$$13 \text{ N} + 8 \text{ N} = 21 \text{ N}$$

The net force is **21 N northwest**.

Forces in Opposite Directions

When forces are in opposite directions, subtract the smaller force from the larger force to determine the net force. The net force will be in the direction of the larger force.

Example:
Calculate the net force on a rope that is being pulled on each end. One person is pulling on one end of the rope with a force of 12 N south. Another person is pulling on the opposite end of the rope with a force of 7 N north.

$$12 \text{ N} - 7 \text{ N} = 5 \text{ N}$$

The net force is **5 N south**.

Pressure

Pressure is the force exerted over a given area. The SI unit for pressure is the pascal. Its symbol is Pa.

$$\text{pressure} = \frac{\text{force}}{\text{area}}$$

Example:
Calculate the pressure of the air in a soccer ball if the air exerts a force of 10 N over an area of 0.5 m^2.

$$\text{pressure} = \frac{10 N}{0.5 \text{ m}^2} = \frac{20 N}{\text{m}^2} = 20 \text{ Pa}$$

The pressure of the air inside the soccer ball is **20 Pa**.

Reading and Study Skills

A How-To Manual for Active Reading

This book belongs to you, and you are invited to write in it. In fact, the book won't be complete until you do. Sometimes you'll answer a question or follow directions to mark up the text. Other times you'll write down your own thoughts. And when you're done reading and writing in the book, the book will be ready to help you review what you learned and prepare for tests.

Active Reading Annotations

Before you read, you'll often come upon an Active Reading prompt that asks you to underline certain words or number the steps in a process. Here's an example.

> ### Active Reading
>
> 12 **Identify** In this paragraph, number the sequence of sentences that describe replication.

Marking the text this way is called **annotating,** and your marks are called **annotations.** Annotating the text can help you identify important concepts while you read.

There are other ways that you can annotate the text. You can draw an asterisk (*) by vocabulary terms, mark unfamiliar or confusing terms and information with a question mark (?), and mark main ideas with a double underline. And you can even invent your own marks to annotate the text!

Other Annotating Opportunities

Keep your pencil, pen, or highlighter nearby as you read, so you can make a note or highlight an important point at any time. Here are a few ideas to get you started.

- Notice the headings in red and blue. The blue headings are questions that point to the main idea of what you're reading. The red headings are answers to the questions in the blue ones. Together these headings outline the content of the lesson. After reading a lesson, you could write your own answers to the questions.

- Notice the bold-faced words that are highlighted in yellow. They are highlighted so that you can easily find them again on the page where they are defined. As you read or as you review, challenge yourself to write your own sentence using the bold-faced term.

- Make a note in the margin at any time. You might
  - Ask a "What if" question
  - Comment on what you read
  - Make a connection to something you read elsewhere
  - Make a logical conclusion from the text

Use your own language and abbreviations. Invent a code, such as using circles and boxes around words to remind you of their importance or relation to each other. Your annotations will help you remember your questions for class discussions, and when you go back to the lesson later, you may be able to fill in what you didn't understand the first time you read it. Like a scientist in the field or in a lab, you will be recording your questions and observations for analysis later.

Active Reading Questions

After you read, you'll often come upon Active Reading questions that ask you to think about what you've just read. You'll write your answer underneath the question. Here's an example.

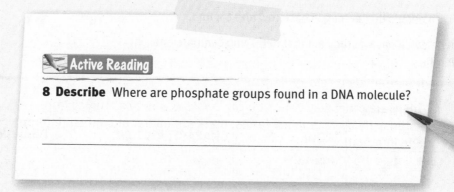

Active Reading

8 Describe Where are phosphate groups found in a DNA molecule?

_____

_____

This type of question helps you sum up what you've just read and pull out the most important ideas from the passage. In this case the question asks you to **describe** the structure of a DNA molecule that you have just read about. Other times you may be asked to do such things as **apply** a concept, **compare** two concepts, **summarize** a process, or **identify a cause-and-effect** relationship. You'll be strengthening those critical thinking skills that you'll use often in learning about science.

Reading and Study Skills

Using Graphic Organizers to Take Notes

Graphic organizers help you remember information as you read it for the first time and as you study it later. There are dozens of graphic organizers to choose from, so the first trick is to choose the one that's best suited to your purpose. Following are some graphic organizers to use for different purposes.

To remember lots of information	To relate a central idea to subordinate details	To describe a process	To make a comparison
• Arrange data in a Content Frame • Use Combination Notes to describe a concept in words and pictures	• Show relationships with a Mind Map or a Main Idea Web • Sum up relationships among many things with a Concept Map	• Use a Process Diagram to explain a procedure • Show a chain of events and results in a Cause-and-Effect Chart	• Compare two or more closely related things in a Venn Diagram

Content Frame

1 Make a four-column chart.

2 Fill the first column with categories (e.g., snail, ant, earthworm) and the first row with descriptive information (e.g., group, characteristic, appearance).

3 Fill the chart with details that belong in each row and column.

4 When you finish, you'll have a study aid that helps you compare one category to another.

Invertebrates

NAME	GROUP	CHARACTERISTICS	DRAWING
snail	mollusks	mangle	
ant	arthropods	six legs, exoskeleton	
earthworm	segmented worms	segmented body, circulatory and digestive systems	
heartworm	roundworms	digestive system	
sea star	echinoderms	spiny skin, tube feet	
jellyfish	cnidarians	stinging cells	

Combination Notes

1 Make a two-column chart.

2 Write descriptive words and definitions in the first column.

3 Draw a simple sketch that helps you remember the meaning of the term in the second column.

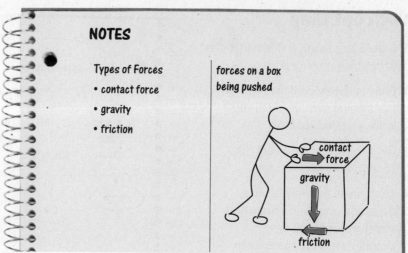

NOTES

Types of Forces
- contact force
- gravity
- friction

forces on a box being pushed

contact force

gravity

friction

Mind Map

1 Draw an oval, and inside it write a topic to analyze.

2 Draw two or more arms extending from the oval. Each arm represents a main idea about the topic.

3 Draw lines from the arms on which to write details about each of the main ideas.

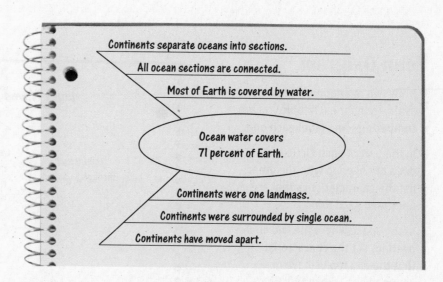

Continents separate oceans into sections.

All ocean sections are connected.

Most of Earth is covered by water.

Ocean water covers 71 percent of Earth.

Continents were one landmass.

Continents were surrounded by single ocean.

Continents have moved apart.

Main Idea Web

1 Make a box and write a concept you want to remember inside it.

2 Draw boxes around the central box, and label each one with a category of information about the concept (e.g., definition, formula, descriptive details).

3 Fill in the boxes with relevant details as you read.

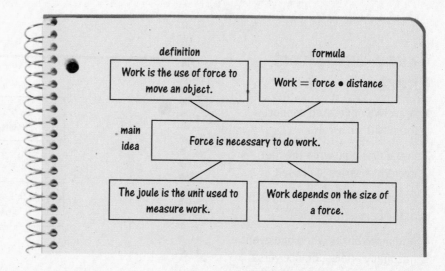

definition

Work is the use of force to move an object.

formula

Work = force • distance

main idea

Force is necessary to do work.

The joule is the unit used to measure work.

Work depends on the size of a force.

Reading and Study Skills

Concept Map

1 Draw a large oval, and inside it write a major concept.

2 Draw an arrow from the concept to a smaller oval, in which you write a related concept.

3 On the arrow, write a verb that connects the two concepts.

4 Continue in this way, adding ovals and arrows in a branching structure, until you have explained as much as you can about the main concept.

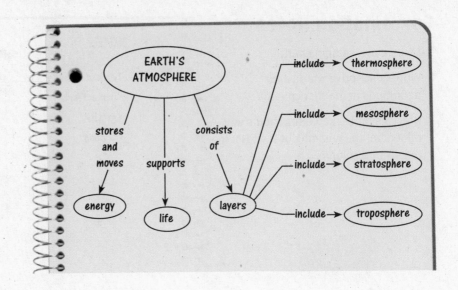

Venn Diagram

1 Draw two overlapping circles or ovals—one for each topic you are comparing—and label each one.

2 In the part of each circle that does not overlap with the other, list the characteristics that are unique to each topic.

3 In the space where the two circles overlap, list the characteristics that the two topics have in common.

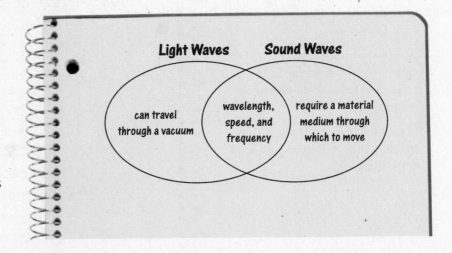

Cause-and-Effect Chart

1 Draw two boxes and connect them with an arrow.

2 In the first box, write the first event in a series (a cause).

3 In the second box, write a result of the cause (the effect).

4 Add more boxes when one event has many effects, or vice versa.

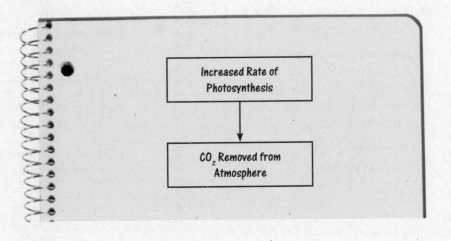

Process Diagram

A process can be a never-ending cycle. As you can see in this technology design process, engineers may backtrack and repeat steps, they may skip steps entirely, or they may repeat the entire process before a useable design is achieved.

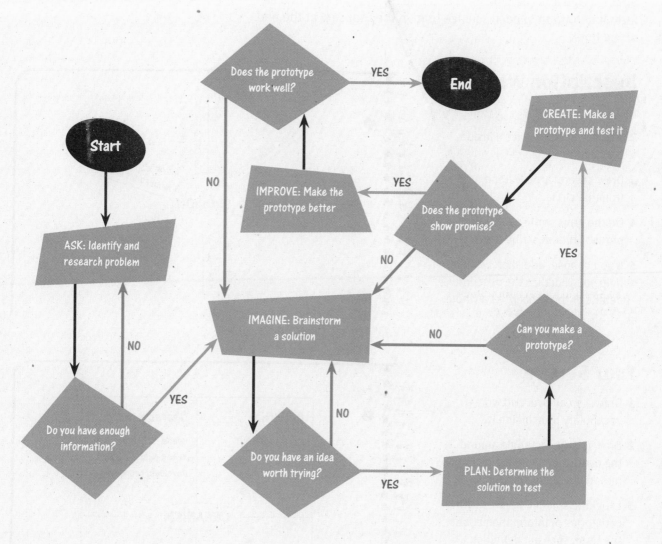

Reading and Study Skills

Using Vocabulary Strategies

Important science terms are highlighted where they are first defined in this book. One way to remember these terms is to take notes and make sketches when you come to them. Use the strategies on this page and the next for this purpose. You will also find a formal definition of each science term in the Glossary at the end of the book.

Description Wheel

1 Draw a small circle.

2 Write a vocabulary term inside the circle.

3 Draw several arms extending from the circle.

4 On the arms, write words and phrases that describe the term.

5 If you choose, add sketches that help you visualize the descriptive details or the concept as a whole.

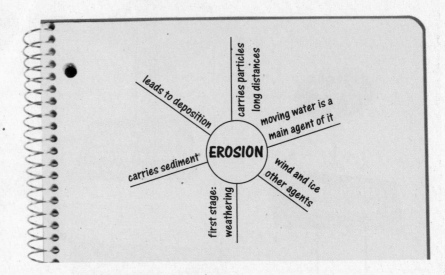

Four Square

1 Draw a small oval and write a vocabulary term inside it.

2 Draw a large rectangle around the oval, and divide the rectangle into four smaller squares.

3 Label the smaller squares with categories of information about the term, such as: definition, characteristics, examples, non-examples, appearance, and root words.

4 Fill the squares with descriptive words and drawings that will help you remember the overall meaning of the term and its essential details.

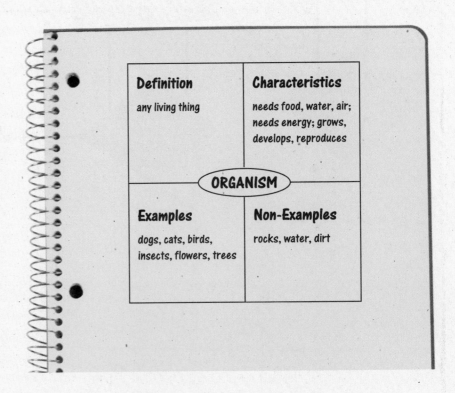

Frame Game

1 Draw a small rectangle, and write a vocabulary term inside it.

2 Draw a larger rectangle around the smaller one. Connect the corners of the larger rectangle to the corners of the smaller one, creating four spaces that frame the word.

3 In each of the four parts of the frame, draw or write details that help define the term. Consider including a definition, essential characteristics, an equation, examples, and a sentence using the term.

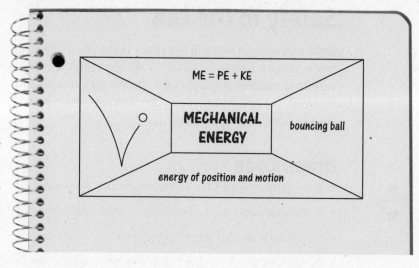

Magnet Word

1 Draw horseshoe magnet, and write a vocabulary term inside it.

2 Add lines that extend from the sides of the magnet.

3 Brainstorm words and phrases that come to mind when you think about the term.

4 On the lines, write the words and phrases that describe something essential about the term.

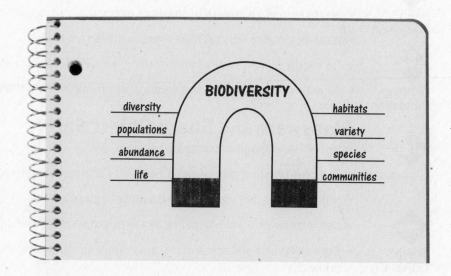

Word Triangle

1 Draw a triangle, and add lines to divide it into three parts.

2 Write a term and its definition in the bottom section of the triangle.

3 In the middle section, write a sentence in which the term is used correctly.

4 In the top section, draw a small picture to illustrate the term.

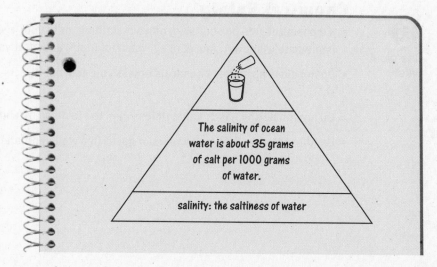

Science Skills

Safety in the Lab

Before you begin work in the laboratory, read these safety rules twice. Before starting a lab activity, read all directions and make sure that you understand them. Do not begin until your teacher has told you to start. If you or another student are injured in any way, tell your teacher immediately.

Dress Code

Eye Protection

Hand Protection

Clothing Protection

- Wear safety goggles at all times in the lab as directed.
- If chemicals get into your eyes, flush your eyes immediately.
- Do not wear contact lenses in the lab.
- Do not look directly at the sun or any intense light source or laser.
- Do not cut an object while holding the object in your hand.
- Wear appropriate protective gloves as directed.
- Wear an apron or lab coat at all times in the lab as directed.
- Tie back long hair, secure loose clothing, and remove loose jewelry.
- Do not wear open-toed shoes, sandals, or canvas shoes in the lab.

Glassware and Sharp Object Safety

Glassware Safety

Sharp Objects Safety

- Do not use chipped or cracked glassware.
- Use heat-resistant glassware for heating or storing hot materials.
- Notify your teacher immediately if a piece of glass breaks.
- Use extreme care when handling all sharp and pointed instruments.
- Cut objects on a suitable surface, always in a direction away from your body.

Chemical Safety

Chemical Safety

- If a chemical gets on your skin, on your clothing, or in your eyes, rinse it immediately (shower, faucet or eyewash fountain) and alert your teacher.
- Do not clean up spilled chemicals unless your teacher directs you to do so.
- Do not inhale any gas or vapor unless directed to do so by your teacher.
- Handle materials that emit vapors or gases in a well-ventilated area.

Electrical Safety

Electrical Safety

- Do not use equipment with frayed electrical cords or loose plugs.
- Do not use electrical equipment near water or when clothing or hands are wet.
- Hold the plug housing when you plug in or unplug equipment.

Heating and Fire Safety

Heating Safety

- Be aware of any source of flames, sparks, or heat (such as flames, heating coils, or hot plates) before working with any flammable substances.
- Know the location of lab fire extinguishers and fire-safety blankets.
- Know your school's fire-evacuation routes.
- If your clothing catches on fire, walk to the lab shower to put out the fire.
- Never leave a hot plate unattended while it is turned on or while it is cooling.
- Use tongs or appropriate insulated holders when handling heated objects.
- Allow all equipment to cool before storing it.

Wafting

Plant and Animal Safety

Plant Safety

Animal Safety

- Do not eat any part of a plant.
- Do not pick any wild plants unless your teacher instructs you to do so.
- Handle animals only as your teacher directs.
- Treat animals carefully and respectfully.
- Wash your hands thoroughly after handling any plant or animal.

Cleanup

Proper Waste Disposal

Hygienic Care

- Clean all work surfaces and protective equipment as directed by your teacher.
- Dispose of hazardous materials or sharp objects only as directed by your teacher.
- Keep your hands away from your face while you are working on any activity.
- Wash your hands thoroughly before you leave the lab or after any activity.

Science Skills

Designing, Conducting, and Reporting an Experiment

An experiment is an organized procedure to study something under specific conditions. Use the following steps of the scientific method when designing or conducting a controlled experiment.

1 Identify a Research Problem

Every day, you make observations by using your senses to gather information. Careful observations lead to good questions, and good questions can lead you to an experiment. Imagine, for example, that you pass a pond every day on your way to school, and you notice green scum beginning to form on top of it. You wonder what it is and why it seems to be growing. You list your questions, and then you do a little research to find out what is already known. A good place to start a research project is at the library. A library catalog lists all of the resources available to you at that library and often those found elsewhere. Begin your search by using:

- keywords or main topics.

- similar words, or synonyms, of your keyword.

The types of resources that will be helpful to you will depend on the kind of information you are interested in. And, some resources are more reliable for a given topic than others. Some different kinds of useful resources are:

- magazines and journals (or periodicals)—articles on a topic.

- encyclopedias—a good overview of a topic.

- books on specific subjects—details about a topic.

- newspapers—useful for current events.

The Internet can also be a great place to find information. Some of your library's reference materials may even be online. When using the Internet, however, it is especially important to make sure you are using appropriate and reliable sources. Websites of universities and government agencies are usually more accurate and reliable than websites created by individuals or businesses. Decide which sources are relevant and reliable for your topic. If in doubt, check with your teacher.

Take notes as you read through the information in these resources. You will probably come up with many questions and ideas for which you can do more research as needed. Once you feel you have enough information, think about the questions you have on the topic. Then, write down the problem that you want to investigate. Your notes might look like these.

© Houghton Mifflin Harcourt Publishing Company

Research Questions	Research Problem	Library and Internet Resources
• How do algae grow? • How do people measure algae? • What kind of fertilizer would affect the growth of algae? • Can fertilizer and algae be used safely in a lab? How?	How does fertilizer affect the algae in a pond?	Pond fertilization: initiating an algal bloom – from University of California Davis website. Blue-Green algae in Wisconsin waters-from the Department of Natural Resources of Wisconsin website.

As you gather information from reliable sources, record details about each source, including author name(s), title, date of publication, and/or web address. Make sure to also note the specific information that you use from each source. Staying organized in this way will be important when you write your report and create a bibliography or works cited list. Recording this information and staying organized will help you credit the appropriate author(s) for the information that you have gathered.

Representing someone else's ideas or work as your own, (without giving the original author credit), is known as plagiarism. Plagiarism can be intentional or unintentional. The best way to make sure that you do not commit plagiarism is to always do your own work and to always give credit to others when you use their words or ideas.

Current scientific research is built on scientific research and discoveries that have happened in the past. This means that scientists are constantly learning from each other and combining ideas to learn more about the natural world through investigation. But, a good scientist always credits the ideas and research that they have gathered from other people to those people. There are more details about crediting sources and creating a bibliography under step 9.

2 Make a Prediction

A prediction is a statement of what you expect will happen in your experiment. Before making a prediction, you need to decide in a general way what you will do in your procedure. You may state your prediction in an if-then format.

Prediction

If the amount of fertilizer in the pond water is increased, then the amount of algae will also increase.

Science Skills

3 Form a Hypothesis

Many experiments are designed to test a hypothesis. A hypothesis is a tentative explanation for an expected result. You have predicted that additional fertilizer will cause additional algae growth in pond water; your hypothesis should state the connection between fertilizer and algal growth.

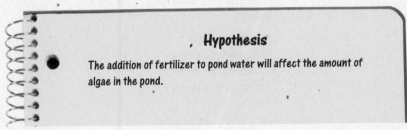

Hypothesis

The addition of fertilizer to pond water will affect the amount of algae in the pond.

4 Identify Variables to Test the Hypothesis

The next step is to design an experiment to test the hypothesis. The experimental results may or may not support the hypothesis. Either way, the information that results from the experiment may be useful for future investigations.

Experimental Group and Control Group

An experiment to determine how two factors are related has a control group and an experimental group. The two groups are the same, except that the investigator changes a single factor in the experimental group and does not change it in the control group.

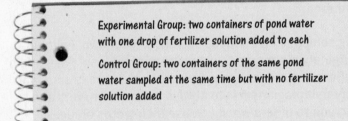

Experimental Group: two containers of pond water with one drop of fertilizer solution added to each

Control Group: two containers of the same pond water sampled at the same time but with no fertilizer solution added

Variables and Constants

In a controlled experiment, a variable is any factor that can change. Constants are all of the variables that are kept the same in both the experimental group and the control group.

The independent variable is the factor that is manipulated or changed in order to test the effect of the change on another variable. The dependent variable is the factor the investigator measures to gather data about the effect.

Independent Variable	Dependent Variable	Constants
Amount of fertilizer in pond water	Growth of algae in the pond water	• Where and when the pond water is obtained • The type of container used • Light and temperature conditions where the water is stored

5 Write a Procedure

Write each step of your procedure. Start each step with a verb, or action word, and keep the steps short. Your procedure should be clear enough for someone else to use as instructions for repeating your experiment.

Procedure

1. Use the masking tape and the marker to label the containers with your initials, the date, and the identifiers "Jar 1 with Fertilizer," "Jar 2 with Fertilizer," "Jar 1 without Fertilizer," and "Jar 2 without Fertilizer."

2. Put on your gloves. Use the large container to obtain a sample of pond water.

3. Divide the water sample equally among the four smaller containers.

4. Use the eyedropper to add one drop of fertilizer solution to the two containers labeled, "Jar 1 with Fertilizer," and "Jar 2 with Fertilizer".

5. Cover the containers with clear plastic wrap. Use the scissors to punch ten holes in each of the covers.

6. Place all four containers on a window ledge. Make sure that they all receive the same amount of light.

7. Observe the containers every day for one week.

8. Use the ruler to measure the diameter of the largest clump of algae in each container, and record your measurements daily.

Science Skills

6 Experiment and Collect Data

Once you have all of your materials and your procedure has been approved, you can begin to experiment and collect data. Record both quantitative data (measurements) and qualitative data (observations), as shown below.

Algal Growth and Fertilizer

Date and Time	Experimental Group		Control Group		Observations
	Jar 1 with Fertilizer (diameter of algal clump in mm)	Jar 2 with Fertilizer (diameter of algal clump in mm)	Jar 1 without Fertilizer (diameter of algal clump in mm)	Jar 2 without Fertilizer (diameter of algal clump in mm)	
5/3 4:00 p.m.	0	0	0	0	condensation in all containers
5/4 4:00 p.m.	0	3	0	0	tiny green blobs in Jar 2 with fertilizer
5/5 4:15 p.m.	4	5	0	3	green blobs in Jars 1 and 2 with fertilizer and Jar 2 without fertilizer
5/6 4:00 p.m.	5	6	0	4	water light green in Jar 2 with fertilizer
5/7 4:00 p.m.	8	10	0	6	water light green in Jars 1 and 2 with fertilizer and Jar 2 without fertilizer
5/8 3:30 p.m.	10	18	0	6	cover off of Jar 2 with fertilizer
5/9 3:30 p.m.	14	23	0	8	drew sketches of each container

Drawings of Samples Viewed Under Microscope on 5/9 at 100x

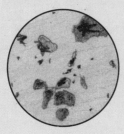

Jar 1 with Fertilizer

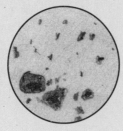

Jar 2 with Fertilizer

Jar 1 without Fertilizer

Jar 2 without Fertilizer

7 Analyze Data

After you complete your experiment, you must analyze all of the data you have gathered. Tables, statistics, and graphs are often used in this step to organize and analyze both the qualitative and quantitative data. Sometimes, your qualitative data are best used to help explain the relationships you see in your quantitative data.

Computer graphing software is useful for creating a graph from data that you have collected. Most graphing software can make line graphs, pie charts, or bar graphs from data that has been organized in a spreadsheet. Graphs are useful for understanding relationships in the data and for communicating the results of your experiment.

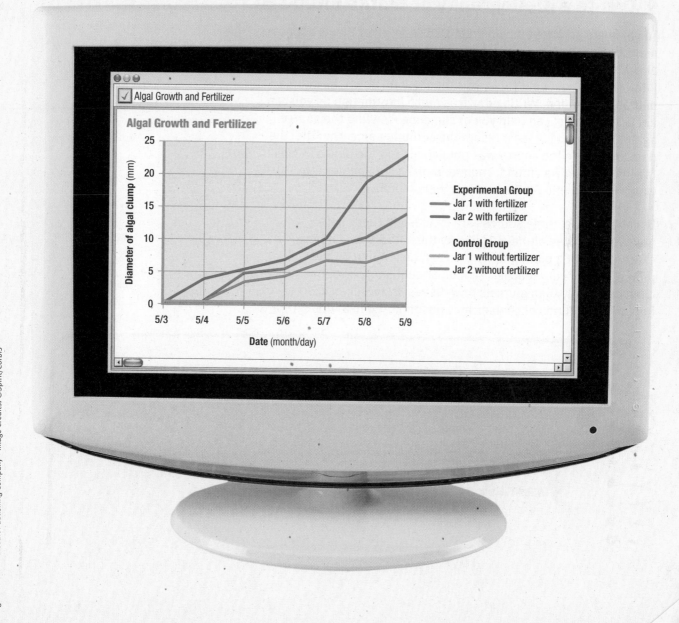

Science Skills

8 Make Conclusions

To draw conclusions from your experiment, first, write your results. Then, compare your results with your hypothesis. Do your results support your hypothesis? What have you learned?

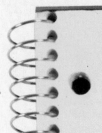

Conclusion

More algae grew in the pond water to which fertilizer had been added than in the pond water to which fertilizer had not been added. My hypothesis was supported. I conclude that it is possible that the growth of algae in ponds can be influenced by the input of fertilizer.

9 Create a Bibliography or Works Cited List

To complete your report, you must also show all of the newspapers, magazines, journals, books, and online sources that you used at every stage of your investigation. Whenever you find useful information about your topic, you should write down the source of that information. Writing down as much information as you can about the subject can help you or someone else find the source again. You should at least record the author's name, the title, the date and where the source was published, and the pages in which the information was found. Then, organize your sources into a list, which you can title Bibliography or Works Cited.

Usually, at least three sources are included in these lists. Sources are listed alphabetically, by the authors' last names. The exact format of a bibliography can vary, depending on the style preferences of your teacher, school, or publisher. Also, books are cited differently than journals or websites. Below is an example of how different kinds of sources may be formatted in a bibliography.

BOOK: Hauschultz, Sara. Freshwater Algae. Brainard, Minnesota: Northwoods Publishing, 2011.

ENCYCLOPEDIA: Lasure, Sedona. "Algae is not all just pond scum." Encyclopedia of Algae. 2009.

JOURNAL: Johnson, Keagan. "Algae as we know it." Sci Journal, vol 64. (September 2010): 201-211.

WEBSITE: Dout, Bill. "Keeping algae scum out of birdbaths." Help Keep Earth Clean. News. January 26, 2011. <www. SaveEarth.org>.

Using a Microscope

Scientists use microscopes to see very small objects that cannot easily be seen with the eye alone. A microscope magnifies the image of an object so that small details may be observed. A microscope that you may use can magnify an object 400 times—the object will appear 400 times larger than its actual size.

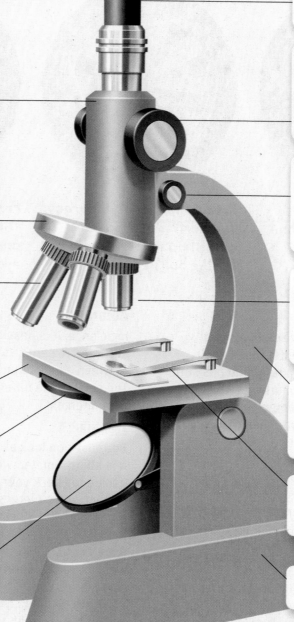

Eyepiece Objects are viewed through the eyepiece. The eyepiece contains a lens that commonly magnifies an image ten times.

Coarse Adjustment This knob is used to focus the image of an object when it is viewed through the low-power lens.

Fine Adjustment This knob is used to focus the image of an object when it is viewed through the high-power lens.

Low-Power Objective Lens This is the smallest lens on the nosepiece. It magnifies images about 10 times.

Arm The arm supports the body above the stage. Always carry a microscope by the arm and base.

Stage Clip The stage clip holds a slide in place on the stage.

Base The base supports the microscope.

Body The body separates the lens in the eyepiece from the objective lenses below.

Nosepiece The nosepiece holds the objective lenses above the stage and rotates so that all lenses may be used.

High-Power Objective Lens This is the largest lens on the nosepiece. It magnifies an image approximately 40 times.

Stage The stage supports the object being viewed.

Diaphragm The diaphragm is used to adjust the amount of light passing through the slide and into an objective lens.

Mirror or Light Source Some microscopes use light that is reflected through the stage by a mirror. Other microscopes have their own light sources.

Science Skills

Measuring Accurately

Precision and Accuracy

When you do a scientific investigation, it is important that your methods, observations, and data be both precise and accurate.

Low precision: The darts did not land in a consistent place on the dartboard.

Precision, but not accuracy: The darts landed in a consistent place, but did not hit the bull's eye.

Precision and accuracy: The darts landed consistently on the bull's eye.

Precision

In science, *precision* is the exactness and consistency of measurements. For example, measurements made with a ruler that has both centimeter and millimeter markings would be more precise than measurements made with a ruler that has only centimeter markings. Another indicator of precision is the care taken to make sure that methods and observations are as exact and consistent as possible. Every time a particular experiment is done, the same procedure should be used. Precision is necessary because experiments are repeated several times and if the procedure changes, the results might change.

Example

Suppose you are measuring temperatures over a two-week period. Your precision will be greater if you measure each temperature at the same place, at the same time of day, and with the same thermometer than if you change any of these factors from one day to the next.

Accuracy

In science, it is possible to be precise but not accurate. *Accuracy* depends on the difference between a measurement and an actual value. The smaller the difference, the more accurate the measurement.

Example

Suppose you look at a stream and estimate that it is about 1 meter wide at a particular place. You decide to check your estimate by measuring the stream with a meter stick, and you determine that the stream is 1.32 meters wide. However, because it is difficult to measure the width of a stream with a meter stick, it turns out that your measurement was not very accurate. The stream is actually 1.14 meters wide. Therefore, even though your estimate of about 1 meter was less precise than your measurement, your estimate was actually more accurate.

Graduated Cylinders

How to Measure the Volume of a Liquid with a Graduated Cylinder

- Be sure that the graduated cylinder is on a flat surface so that your measurement will be accurate.

- When reading the scale on a graduated cylinder, be sure to have your eyes at the level of the surface of the liquid.

- The surface of the liquid will be curved in the graduated cylinder. Read the volume of the liquid at the bottom of the curve, or meniscus (muh-NIHS-kuhs).

- You can use a graduated cylinder to find the volume of a solid object by measuring the increase in a liquid's level after you add the object to the cylinder.

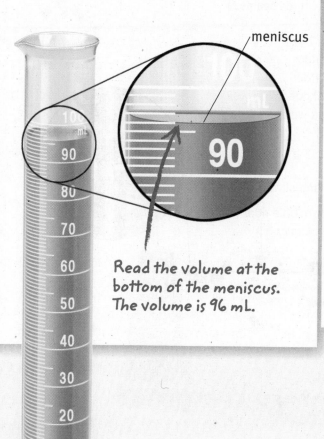

meniscus

Read the volume at the bottom of the meniscus. The volume is 96 mL.

Metric Rulers

How to Measure the Length of a Leaf with a Metric Ruler

1 Lay a ruler flat on top of the leaf so that the 1-centimeter mark lines up with one end. Make sure the ruler and the leaf do not move between the time you line them up and the time you take the measurement.

2 Look straight down on the ruler so that you can see exactly how the marks line up with the other end of the leaf.

3 Estimate the length by which the leaf extends beyond a marking. For example, the leaf below extends about halfway between the 4.2-centimeter and 4.3-centimeter marks, so the apparent measurement is about 4.25 centimeters.

4 Remember to subtract 1 centimeter from your apparent measurement, since you started at the 1-centimeter mark on the ruler and not at the end. The leaf is about 3.25 centimeters long (4.25 cm − 1 cm = 3.25 cm).

Triple Beam Balance

This balance has a pan and three beams with sliding masses, called riders. At one end of the beams is a pointer that indicates whether the mass on the pan is equal to the masses shown on the beams.

How to Measure the Mass of an Object

1. Make sure the balance is zeroed before measuring the mass of an object. The balance is zeroed if the pointer is at zero when nothing is on the pan and the riders are at their zero points. Use the adjustment knob at the base of the balance to zero it.

2. Place the object to be measured on the pan.

3. Move the riders one notch at a time away from the pan. Begin with the largest rider. If moving the largest rider one notch brings the pointer below zero, begin measuring the mass of the object with the next smaller rider.

4. Change the positions of the riders until they balance the mass on the pan and the pointer is at zero. Then add the readings from the three beams to determine the mass of the object.

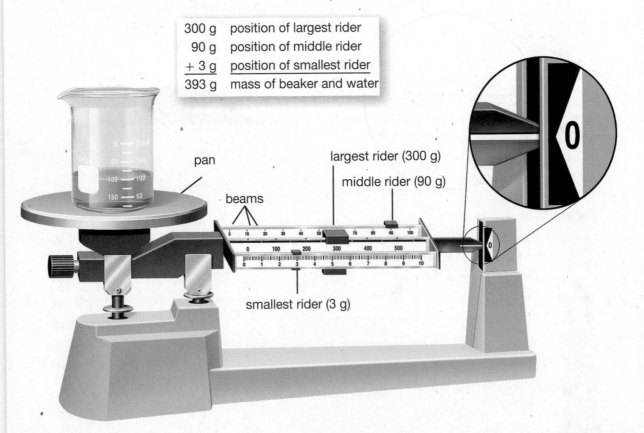

300 g	position of largest rider
90 g	position of middle rider
+ 3 g	position of smallest rider
393 g	mass of beaker and water

pan

beams

largest rider (300 g)

middle rider (90 g)

smallest rider (3 g)

Using the Metric System and SI Units

Scientists use International System (SI) units for measurements of distance, volume, mass, and temperature. The International System is based on powers of ten and the metric system of measurement.

Basic SI Units		
Quantity	Name	Symbol
length	meter	m
volume	liter	L
mass	gram	g
temperature	kelvin	K

SI Prefixes		
Prefix	Symbol	Power of 10
kilo-	k	1000
hecto-	h	100
deca-	da	10
deci-	d	0.1 or $\frac{1}{10}$
centi-	c	0.01 or $\frac{1}{100}$
milli-	m	0.001 or $\frac{1}{1000}$

Changing Metric Units

You can change from one unit to another in the metric system by multiplying or dividing by a power of 10.

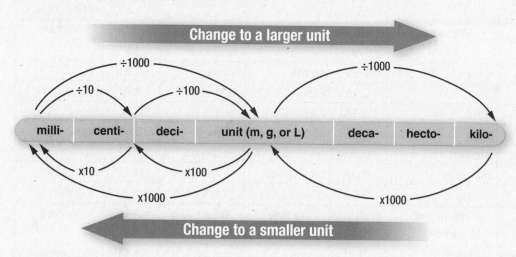

Change to a larger unit

÷1000 ÷10 ÷100 ÷1000

milli- | centi- | deci- | unit (m, g, or L) | deca- | hecto- | kilo-

x10 x100 x1000 x1000

Change to a smaller unit

Example

Change 0.64 liters to milliliters.
1 Decide whether to multiply or divide.
2 Select the power of 10.

Change to a smaller unit by multiplying

mL ◄— x 1000 — L

0.64 x 1000 = 640.

ANSWER 0.64 L = 640 mL

Example

Change 23.6 grams to kilograms.
1 Decide whether to multiply or divide.
2 Select the power of 10.

Change to a larger unit by dividing

g — ÷ 1000 —► kg

26.3 ÷ 1000 = 0.0263

ANSWER 23.6 g = 0.0236 kg

Science Skills

Converting Between SI and U.S. Customary Units

Use the chart below when you need to convert between SI units and U.S. customary units.

SI Unit	From SI to U.S. Customary			From U.S. Customary to SI		
Length	**When you know**	**multiply by**	**to find**	**When you know**	**multiply by**	**to find**
kilometer (km) = 1000 m	kilometers	0.62	miles	miles	1.61	kilometers
meter (m) = 100 cm	meters	3.28	feet	feet	0.3048	meters
centimeter (cm) = 10 mm	centimeters	0.39	inches	inches	2.54	centimeters
millimeter (mm) = 0.1 cm	millimeters	0.04	inches	inches	25.4	millimeters
Area	**When you know**	**multiply by**	**to find**	**When you know**	**multiply by**	**to find**
square kilometer (km²)	square kilometers	0.39	square miles	square miles	2.59	square kilometers
square meter (m²)	square meters	1.2	square yards	square yards	0.84	square meters
square centimeter (cm²)	square centimeters	0.155	square inches	square inches	6.45	square centimeters
Volume	**When you know**	**multiply by**	**to find**	**When you know**	**multiply by**	**to find**
liter (L) = 1000 mL	liters	1.06	quarts	quarts	0.95	liters
	liters	0.26	gallons	gallons	3.79	liters
	liters	4.23	cups	cups	0.24	liters
	liters	2.12	pints	pints	0.47	liters
milliliter (mL) = 0.001 L	milliliters	0.20	teaspoons	teaspoons	4.93	milliliters
	milliliters	0.07	tablespoons	tablespoons	14.79	milliliters
	milliliters	0.03	fluid ounces	fluid ounces	29.57	milliliters
Mass	**When you know**	**multiply by**	**to find**	**When you know**	**multiply by**	**to find**
kilogram (kg) = 1000 g	kilograms	2.2	pounds	pounds	0.45	kilograms
gram (g) = 1000 mg	grams	0.035	ounces	ounces	28.35	grams

Temperature Conversions

Even though the kelvin is the SI base unit of temperature, the degree Celsius will be the unit you use most often in your science studies. The formulas below show the relationships between temperatures in degrees Fahrenheit (°F), degrees Celsius (°C), and kelvins (K).

$$°C = \frac{5}{9} \ (°F - 32) \qquad °F = \frac{9}{5} \ °C + 32 \qquad K = °C + 273$$

Examples of Temperature Conversions		
Condition	**Degrees Celsius**	**Degrees Fahrenheit**
Freezing point of water	0	32
Cool day	10	50
Mild day	20	68
Warm day	30	86
Normal body temperature	37	98.6
Very hot day	40	104
Boiling point of water	100	212

Math Refresher

Performing Calculations

Science requires an understanding of many math concepts. The following pages will help you review some important math skills.

Mean

The mean is the sum of all values in a data set divided by the total number of values in the data set. The mean is also called the *average*.

Example

Find the mean of the following set of numbers: 5, 4, 7, and 8.

Step 1   Find the sum.

$$5 + 4 + 7 + 8 = 24$$

Step 2   Divide the sum by the number of numbers in your set. Because there are four numbers in this example, divide the sum by 4.

$$24 ÷ 4 = 6$$

Answer The average, or mean, is 6.

Median

The median of a data set is the middle value when the values are written in numerical order. If a data set has an even number of values, the median is the mean of the two middle values.

Example

To find the median of a set of measurements, arrange the values in order from least to greatest. The median is the middle value.

     13 mm   14 mm   16 mm   21 mm   23 mm

Answer The median is 16 mm.

Mode

The mode of a data set is the value that occurs most often.

Example

To find the mode of a set of measurements, arrange the values in order from least to greatest and determine the value that occurs most often.

     13 mm, 14 mm, 14 mm, 16 mm,
     21 mm, 23 mm, 25 mm

Answer The mode is 14 mm.

A data set can have more than one mode or no mode. For example, the following data set has modes of 2 mm and 4 mm:

     2 mm   2 mm   3 mm   4 mm   4 mm

The data set below has no mode, because no value occurs more often than any other.

     2 mm   3 mm   4 mm   5 mm

Math Refresher

Ratios

A **ratio** is a comparison between numbers, and it is usually written as a fraction.

Example

Find the ratio of thermometers to students if you have 36 thermometers and 48 students in your class.

Step 1   Write the ratio.

$$\frac{36 \text{ thermometers}}{48 \text{ students}}$$

Step 2   Simplify the fraction to its simplest form.

$$\frac{36}{48} = \frac{36 \div 12}{48 \div 12} = \frac{3}{4}$$

The ratio of thermometers to students is 3 to 4 or 3:4.

Proportions

A **proportion** is an equation that states that two ratios are equal.

$$\frac{3}{1} = \frac{12}{4}$$

To solve a proportion, you can use cross-multiplication. If you know three of the quantities in a proportion, you can use cross-multiplication to find the fourth.

Example

Imagine that you are making a scale model of the solar system for your science project. The diameter of Jupiter is 11.2 times the diameter of the Earth. If you are using a plastic-foam ball that has a diameter of 2 cm to represent the Earth, what must the diameter of the ball representing Jupiter be?

$$\frac{11.2}{1} = \frac{x}{2 \text{ cm}}$$

Step 1   Cross-multiply.

$$\frac{11.2}{1} = \frac{x}{2}$$

$$11.2 \times 2 = x \times 1$$

Step 2   Multiply.

$$22.4 = x \times 1$$

$$x = 22.4 \text{ cm}$$

You will need to use a ball that has a diameter of 22.4 cm to represent Jupiter.

Rates

A **rate** is a ratio of two values expressed in different units. A unit rate is a rate with a denominator of 1 unit.

Example

A plant grew 6 centimeters in 2 days. The plant's rate of growth was $\frac{6 \text{ cm}}{2 \text{ days}}$.

To describe the plant's growth in centimeters per day, write a unit rate.

Divide numerator and denominator by 2:

$$\frac{6 \text{ cm}}{2 \text{ days}} = \frac{6 \text{ cm} \div 2}{2 \text{ days} \div 2}$$

Simplify:

$$= \frac{3 \text{ cm}}{1 \text{ day}}$$

Answer   The plant's rate of growth is 3 centimeters per day.

Percent

A **percent** is a ratio of a given number to 100. For example, 85% = 85/100. You can use percent to find part of a whole.

Example
What is 85% of 40?

Step 1 Rewrite the percent as a decimal by moving the decimal point two places to the left.

$$0.85$$

Step 2 Multiply the decimal by the number that you are calculating the percentage of.

$$0.85 \times 40 = 34$$

85% of 40 is 34.

Decimals

To **add** or **subtract decimals**, line up the digits vertically so that the decimal points line up. Then, add or subtract the columns from right to left. Carry or borrow numbers as necessary.

Example
Add the following numbers: 3.1415 and 2.96.

Step 1 Line up the digits vertically so that the decimal points line up.

$$\begin{array}{r} 3.1415 \\ + 2.96 \\ \hline \end{array}$$

Step 2 Add the columns from right to left, and carry when necessary.

$$\begin{array}{r} 3.1415 \\ + 2.96 \\ \hline 6.1015 \end{array}$$

The sum is 6.1015.

Fractions

A **fraction** is a ratio of two nonzero whole numbers.

Example
Your class has 24 plants. Your teacher instructs you to put 5 plants in a shady spot. What fraction of the plants in your class will you put in a shady spot?

Step 1 In the denominator, write the total number of parts in the whole.

$$\frac{?}{24}$$

Step 2 In the numerator, write the number of parts of the whole that are being considered.

$$\frac{5}{24}$$

So, $\frac{5}{24}$ of the plants will be in the shade.

Math Refresher

Simplifying Fractions

It is usually best to express a fraction in its simplest form.
Expressing a fraction in its simplest form is called **simplifying
a fraction**.

Example

Simplify the fraction $\frac{30}{45}$ to its simplest form.

Step 1   Find the largest whole number that will divide evenly into
both the numerator and denominator. This number is called
the greatest common factor (GCF).

Factors of the numerator 30:
1, 2, 3, 5, 6, 10, 15, 30

Factors of the denominator 45:
1, 3, 5, 9, 15, 45

Step 2   Divide both the numerator and the denominator by the
GCF, which in this case is 15.

$$\frac{30}{45} = \frac{30 \div 15}{45 \div 15} = \frac{2}{3}$$

Thus, $\frac{30}{45}$ written in its simplest form is $\frac{2}{3}$.

Adding and Subtracting Fractions

To **add** or **subtract fractions** that have the
same denominator, simply add or subtract the
numerators.

Examples

$\frac{3}{5} + \frac{1}{5} = ?$ and $\frac{3}{4} - \frac{1}{4} = ?$

Step 1   Add or subtract the numerators.

$$\frac{3}{5} + \frac{1}{5} = \frac{4}{} \text{ and } \frac{3}{4} - \frac{1}{4} = \frac{2}{}$$

Step 2   Write in the common denominator, which remains the same.

$$\frac{3}{5} + \frac{1}{5} = \frac{4}{5} \text{ and } \frac{3}{4} - \frac{1}{4} = \frac{2}{4}$$

Step 3   If necessary, write the fraction in its simplest form.

$\frac{4}{5}$ cannot be simplified, and $\frac{2}{4} = \frac{1}{2}$.

To **add** or **subtract** fractions that have **different
denominators**, first find the least common
denominator (LCD).

Examples

$\frac{1}{2} + \frac{1}{6} = ?$ and $\frac{3}{4} - \frac{2}{3} = ?$

Step 1   Write the equivalent fractions that have a common
denominator.

$$\frac{3}{6} + \frac{1}{6} = ? \text{ and } \frac{9}{12} - \frac{8}{12} = ?$$

Step 2   Add or subtract the fractions.

$$\frac{3}{6} + \frac{1}{6} = \frac{4}{6} \text{ and } \frac{9}{12} - \frac{8}{12} = \frac{1}{12}$$

Step 3   If necessary, write the fraction in its simplest form.

$\frac{4}{6} = \frac{2}{3}$, and $\frac{1}{12}$ cannot be simplifed.

Multiplying Fractions

To **multiply fractions**, multiply the numerators and the denominators
together, and then simplify the fraction to its simplest form.

Example

$\frac{5}{9} \times \frac{7}{10} = ?$

Step 1   Multiply the numerators and denominators.

$$\frac{5}{9} \times \frac{7}{10} = \frac{5 \times 7}{9 \times 10} = \frac{35}{90}$$

Step 2   Simplify the fraction.

$$\frac{35}{90} = \frac{35 \div 5}{90 \div 5} = \frac{7}{18}$$

Dividing Fractions

To **divide fractions,** first rewrite the divisor (the number you divide by) upside down. This number is called the reciprocal of the divisor. Then multiply and simplify if necessary.

Example

$$\frac{5}{8} \div \frac{3}{2} = ?$$

Step 1 Rewrite the divisor as its reciprocal.

$$\frac{3}{2} \rightarrow \frac{2}{3}$$

Step 2 Multiply the fractions.

$$\frac{5}{8} \times \frac{2}{3} = \frac{5 \times 2}{8 \times 3} = \frac{10}{24}$$

Step 3 Simplify the fraction.

$$\frac{10}{24} = \frac{10 \div 2}{24 \div 2} = \frac{5}{12}$$

Using Significant Figures

The **significant figures** in a decimal are the digits that are warranted by the accuracy of a measuring device.

When you perform a calculation with measurements, the number of significant figures to include in the result depends in part on the number of significant figures in the measurements. When you multiply or divide measurements, your answer should have only as many significant figures as the measurement with the fewest significant figures.

Examples

Using a balance and a graduated cylinder filled with water, you determined that a marble has a mass of 8.0 grams and a volume of 3.5 cubic centimeters. To calculate the density of the marble, divide the mass by the volume.

Write the formula for density: $\text{Density} = \dfrac{\text{mass}}{\text{volume}}$

Substitute measurements: $= \dfrac{8.0 \text{ g}}{3.5 \text{ cm}^3}$

Use a calculator to divide: $\approx 2.285714286 \text{ g/cm}^3$

Answer Because the mass and the volume have two significant figures each, give the density to two significant figures. The marble has a density of 2.3 grams per cubic centimeter.

Using Scientific Notation

Scientific notation is a shorthand way to write very large or very small numbers. For example, 73,500,000,000,000,000,000,000 kg is the mass of the moon. In scientific notation, it is 7.35×10^{22} kg. A value written as a number between 1 and 10, times a power of 10, is in scientific notation.

Examples

You can convert from standard form to scientific notation.

Standard Form	Scientific Notation
720,000	7.2×10^5
5 decimal places left	Exponent is 5.
0.000291	2.91×10^{-4}
4 decimal places right	Exponent is −4.

You can convert from scientific notation to standard form.

Scientific Notation	Standard Form
4.63×10^7	46,300,000
Exponent is 7.	7 decimal places right
1.08×10^{-6}	0.00000108
Exponent is −6.	6 decimal places left

Math Refresher

Making and Interpreting Graphs

Circle Graph

A circle graph, or pie chart, shows how each group of data relates to all of the data. Each part of the circle represents a category of the data. The entire circle represents all of the data. For example, a biologist studying a hardwood forest in Wisconsin found that there were five different types of trees. The data table at right summarizes the biologist's findings.

Wisconsin Hardwood Trees	
Type of tree	**Number found**
Oak	600
Maple	750
Beech	300
Birch	1,200
Hickory	150
Total	3,000

How to Make a Circle Graph

1 To make a circle graph of these data, first find the percentage of each type of tree. Divide the number of trees of each type by the total number of trees, and multiply by 100%.

$$\frac{600 \text{ oak}}{3,000 \text{ trees}} \times 100\% = 20\%$$

$$\frac{750 \text{ maple}}{3,000 \text{ trees}} \times 100\% = 25\%$$

$$\frac{300 \text{ beech}}{3,000 \text{ trees}} \times 100\% = 10\%$$

$$\frac{1,200 \text{ birch}}{3,000 \text{ trees}} \times 100\% = 40\%$$

$$\frac{150 \text{ hickory}}{3,000 \text{ trees}} \times 100\% = 5\%$$

2 Now, determine the size of the wedges that make up the graph. Multiply each percentage by 360°. Remember that a circle contains 360°.

$$20\% \times 360° = 72° \qquad 25\% \times 360° = 90°$$

$$10\% \times 360° = 36° \qquad 40\% \times 360° = 144°$$

$$5\% \times 360° = 18°$$

3 Check that the sum of the percentages is 100 and the sum of the degrees is 360.

$$20\% + 25\% + 10\% + 40\% + 5\% = 100\%$$

$$72° + 90° + 36° + 144° + 18° = 360°$$

4 Use a compass to draw a circle and mark the center of the circle.

5 Then, use a protractor to draw angles of 72°, 90°, 36°, 144°, and 18° in the circle.

6 Finally, label each part of the graph, and choose an appropriate title.

A Community of Wisconsin Hardwood Trees

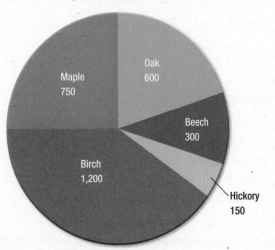

Line Graphs

Line graphs are most often used to demonstrate continuous change. For example, Mr. Smith's students analyzed the population records for their hometown, Appleton, between 1910 and 2010. Examine the data at right.

   Because the year and the population change, they are the variables. The population is determined by, or dependent on, the year. Therefore, the population is called the **dependent variable,** and the year is called the **independent variable**. Each year and its population make a **data pair**. To prepare a line graph, you must first organize data pairs into a table like the one at right.

Population of Appleton, 1910–2010	
Year	**Population**
1910	1,800
1930	2,500
1950	3,200
1970	3,900
1990	4,600
2010	5,300

How to Make a Line Graph

1 Place the independent variable along the horizontal (*x*) axis. Place the dependent variable along the vertical (*y*) axis.

2 Label the *x*-axis "Year" and the *y*-axis "Population." Look at your greatest and least values for the population. For the *y*-axis, determine a scale that will provide enough space to show these values. You must use the same scale for the entire length of the axis. Next, find an appropriate scale for the *x*-axis.

3 Choose reasonable starting points for each axis.

4 Plot the data pairs as accurately as possible.

5 Choose a title that accurately represents the data.

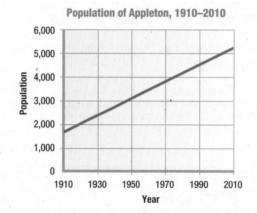

How to Determine Slope

Slope is the ratio of the change in the *y*-value to the change in the x-value, or "rise over run."

1 Choose two points on the line graph. For example, the population of Appleton in 2010 was 5,300 people. Therefore, you can define point A as (2010, 5,300). In 1910, the population was 1,800 people. You can define point B as (1910, 1,800).

2 Find the change in the *y*-value.
(*y* at point A) − (*y* at point B) =
5,300 people − 1,800 people =
3,500 people

3 Find the change in the *x*-value.
(*x* at point A) − (*x* at point B) =
2010 − 1910 = 100 years

4 Calculate the slope of the graph by dividing the change in *y* by the change in *x*.

$$slope = \frac{change\ in\ y}{change\ in\ x}$$

$$slope = \frac{3,500\ people}{100\ years}$$

$$slope = 35\ people\ per\ year$$

In this example, the population in Appleton increased by a fixed amount each year. The graph of these data is a straight line. Therefore, the relationship is **linear**. When the graph of a set of data is not a straight line, the relationship is **nonlinear**.

Math Refresher

Bar Graphs

Bar graphs can be used to demonstrate change that is not continuous. These graphs can be used to indicate trends when the data cover a long period of time. A meteorologist gathered the precipitation data shown here for Summerville for April 1–15 and used a bar graph to represent the data.

Precipitation in Summerville, April 1–15			
Date	Precipitation (cm)	Date	Precipitation (cm)
April 1	0.5	April 9	0.25
April 2	1.25	April 10	0.0
April 3	0.0	April 11	1.0
April 4	0.0	April 12	0.0
April 5	0.0	April 13	0.25
April 6	0.0	April 14	0.0
April 7	0.0	April 15	6.50
April 8	1.75		

How to Make a Bar Graph

1 Use an appropriate scale and a reasonable starting point for each axis.

2 Label the axes, and plot the data.

3 Choose a title that accurately represents the data.

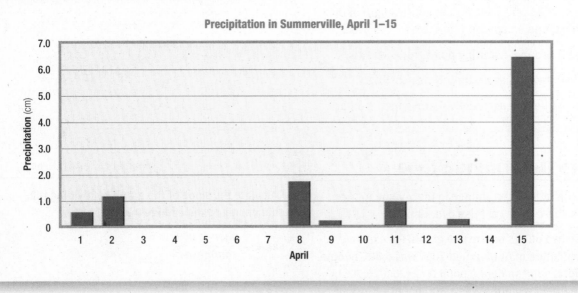

Precipitation in Summerville, April 1–15

Glossary

Pronunciation Key							
Sound	**Symbol**	**Example**	**Respelling**	**Sound**	**Symbol**	**Example**	**Respelling**
ă	a	pat	PAT	ŏ	ah	bottle	BAHT'l
ā	ay	pay	PAY	ō	oh	toe	TOH
âr	air	care	KAIR	ô	aw	caught	KAWT
ä	ah	father	FAH•ther	ôr	ohr	roar	ROHR
är	ar	argue	AR•gyoo	oi	oy	noisy	NOYZ•ee
ch	ch	chase	CHAYS	ŏŏ	u	book	BUK
ĕ	e	pet	PET	ōō	oo	boot	BOOT
ĕ (at end of a syllable)	eh	settee lessee	seh•TEE leh•SEE	ou	ow	pound	POWND
ĕr	ehr	merry	MEHR•ee	s	s	center	SEN•ter
ē	ee	beach	BEECH	sh	sh	cache	CASH
g	g	gas	GAS	ŭ	uh	flood	FLUHD
ĭ	i	pit	PIT	ûr	er	bird	BERD
ĭ (at end of a syllable)	ih	guitar	gih•TAR	z	z	xylophone	ZY•luh•fohn
				z	z	bags	BAGZ
ī	y eye (only for a complete syllable)	pie island	PY EYE•luhnd	zh	zh	decision	dih•SIZH•uhn
				ə	uh	around broken focus	uh•ROWND BROH•kuhn FOH•kuhs
îr	ir	hear	HIR	ər	er	winner	WIN•er
j	j	germ	JERM	th	th	thin they	THIN THAY
k	k	kick	KIK				
ng	ng	thing	THING	w	w	one	WUHN
ngk	ngk	bank	BANGK	wh	hw	whether	HWETH•er

A

adaptation (ad·ap·TAY·shuhn) a characteristic that improves an individual's ability to survive and reproduce in a particular environment (21)
adaptación una característica que mejora la capacidad de un individuo para sobrevivir y reproducirse en un determinado ambiente

algae (AL·jee) eukaryotic organisms that convert the sun's energy into food through photosynthesis but that do not have roots, stems, or leaves (singular, alga) (99)
algas organismos eucarióticos que transforman la energía del Sol en alimento por medio de la fotosíntesis, pero que no tienen raíces, tallos ni hojas

angiosperm (AN·jee·uh·sperm) a flowering plant that produces seeds within a fruit (115)
angiosperma una planta que da flores y que produce semillas dentro de la fruta

Animalia (an·uh·MAYL·yuh) a kingdom made up of complex, multicellular organisms that lack cell walls, can usually move around, and quickly respond to their environment (61)
Animalia un reino formado por organismos pluricelulares complejos que no tienen pared celular, normalmente son capaces de moverse y reaccionan rápidamente a su ambiente

Archaea (ar·KEE·uh) a domain made up of prokaryotes, most of which are known to live in extreme environments, that are distinguished from other prokaryotes by differences in their genetics and in the makeup of their cell wall (58, 80)
Archaea un dominio compuesto por procariotes la mayoría de los cuales viven en ambientes extremos que se distinguen de otros procariotes por su genética y por la composición de su pared celular

artificial selection (ar·tuh·FISH·uhl sih·LEK·shuhn) the human practice of breeding animals or plants that have certain desired traits (18)
selección artificial la práctica humana de criar animales o cultivar plantas que tienen ciertos caracteres deseados

asexual reproduction (ay·SEK·shoo·uhl ree·pruh·DUHK·shuhn) reproduction that does not involve the union of sex cells and in which one parent produces offspring that are genetically identical to the parent (8)
reproducción asexual reproducción que no involucra la unión de células sexuales, en la que un solo progenitor produce descendencia que es genéticamente igual al progenitor

B

Bacteria (bak·TIR·ee·uh) a domain made up of prokaryotes that usually have a cell wall and that usually reproduce by cell division (58, 80)
Bacteria un dominio compuesto por procariotes que por lo general tienen pared celular y se reproducen por división celular

binary fission (BY·nuh·ree FISH·uhn) a form of asexual reproduction in single-celled organisms by which one cell divides into two cells of the same size (84)
fisión binaria una forma de reproducción asexual de los organismos unicelulares, por medio de la cual la célula se divide en dos células del mismo tamaño

C

cell (SEL) in biology, the smallest unit that can perform all life processes; cells are covered by a membrane and contain DNA and cytoplasm (6)
célula en biología, la unidad más pequeña que puede realizar todos los procesos vitales; las células están cubiertas por una membrana y tienen ADN y citoplasma

cellular respiration (SEL·yuh·luhr res·puh·RAY·shuhn) the process by which cells use oxygen to produce energy from food (123)
respiración celular el proceso por medio del cual las células utilizan oxígeno para producir energía a partir de los alimentos

chlorophyll (KLOHR·uh·fil) a green pigment that captures light energy for photosynthesis (109)
clorofila un pigmento verde que capta la energía luminosa para la fotosíntesis

consumer (kuhn·SOO·mer) an organism that eats other organisms or organic matter (141)
consumidor un organismo que se alimenta de otros organismos o de materia orgánica

D

dichotomous key (dy·KAHT·uh·muhs KEE) an aid that is used to identify organisms and that consists of the answers to a series of questions (64)
clave dicotómica una ayuda para identificar organismos, que consiste en las respuestas a una serie de preguntas

DNA (dee·en·AY) deoxyribonucleic acid, a molecule that is present in all living cells and that contains the information that determines the traits that a living thing inherits and needs to live (8)

ADN ácido desoxirribonucleico, una molécula que está presente en todas las células vivas y que contiene la información que determina los caracteres que un ser vivo hereda y necesita para vivir

domain (doh·MAYN) in a taxonomic system, one of the three broad groups that all living things fall into (58)

dominio en un sistema taxonómico, uno de los tres amplios grupos al que pertenecen todos los seres vivos

dormant (DOHR·muhnt) describes the inactive state of a seed or other plant part when conditions are unfavorable to growth (130)

aletargado término que describe el estado inactivo de una semilla u otra parte de las plantas cuando las condiciones son desfavorables para el crecimiento

endoskeleton (en·doh·SKEL·ih·tn) an internal skeleton made of bone and cartilage (143)

endoesqueleto un esqueleto interno hecho de hueso y cartílago

estivation (es·tuh·VAY·shuhn) a period of inactivity and lowered body temperature that some animals undergo in summer as a protection against hot weather and lack of food (157)

estivación un período de inactividad y menor temperatura corporal por el que pasan algunos animales durante el verano para protegerse del calor y la falta de alimento

Eukarya (yoo·KAIR·ee·uh) in a modern taxonomic system, a domain made up of all eukaryotes; this domain aligns with the traditional kingdoms Protista, Fungi, Plantae, and Animalia (59)

Eukarya en un sistema taxonómico moderno, un dominio compuesto por todos los eucariotes; este dominio coincide con los reinos tradicionales Protista, Fungi, Plantae y Animalia

evolution (ev·uh·LOO·shuhn) the process in which inherited characteristics within a population change over generations such that new species sometimes arise (16)

evolución el proceso por medio del cual las características heredadas dentro de una población cambian con el transcurso de las generaciones de manera tal que a veces surgen nuevas especies

exoskeleton (ek·soh·SKEL·ih·tn) a hard, external, supporting structure (143)

exoesqueleto una estructura de soporte, dura y externa

extinction (ek·STINGK·shuhn) the death of every member of a species (23, 31, 41)

extinción la muerte de todos los miembros de una especie

fossil (FAHS·uhl) the trace or remains of an organism that lived long ago, most commonly preserved in sedimentary rock (31, 40)

fósil los indicios o los restos de un organismo que vivió hace mucho tiempo, comúnmente preservados en las rocas sedimentarias

fossil record (FAHS·uhl REK·erd) the history of life in the geologic past as indicated by the traces or remains of living things (31, 40)

registro fósil la historia de la vida en el pasado geológico según la indican los rastros o restos de seres vivos

Fungi (FUHN·jy) a kingdom made up of nongreen, eukaryotic organisms that have no means of movement, reproduce by using spores, and get food by breaking down substances in their surroundings and absorbing the nutrients (60, 100)

Fungi un reino formado por organismos eucarióticos no verdes que no tienen capacidad de movimiento, se reproducen por esporas y obtienen alimento al descomponer sustancias de su entorno y absorber los nutrientes

gamete (GAM·eet) a haploid reproductive cell that unites with another haploid reproductive cell to form a zygote (97)

gameto una célula reproductiva haploide que se une con otra célula reproductiva haploide para formar un cigoto

genus (JEE·nuhs) the level of classification that comes after family and that contains similar species (56)

género el nivel de clasificación que viene después de la familia y que contiene especies similares

geologic time scale (jee·uh·LAHJ·ik TYM SKAYL) the standard method used to divide Earth's long natural history into manageable parts (42)

escala de tiempo geológico el método estándar que se usa para dividir la larga historia natural de la Tierra en partes razonables

gymnosperm (JIM·nuh·sperm) a woody, vascular seed plant whose seeds are not enclosed by an ovary or fruit (114)

gimnosperma una planta leñosa vascular que produce semillas que no están contenidas en un ovario o fruto

hibernation (hy·buhr·NAY·shuhn) a period of inactivity and lowered body temperature that some animals undergo in winter as a protection against cold weather and lack of food (157)
hibernación un período de inactividad y disminución de la temperatura del cuerpo que algunos animales experimentan en invierno como protección contra el tiempo frío y la escasez de comida

homeostasis (hoh·mee·oh·STAY·sis) the maintenance of a constant internal state in a changing environment (7)
homeostasis la capacidad de mantener un estado interno constante en un ambiente en cambio

host (HOHST) an organism from which a parasite takes food or shelter (88)
huésped el organismo del cual un parásito obtiene alimento y refugio

hypha (HY·fuh) a nonreproductive filament of a fungus (100)
hifa un filamento no-reproductor de un hongo

innate behavior (ih·NAYT bih·HAYV·yer) an inherited behavior that does not depend on the environment or experience (153)
conducta innata una conducta heredada que no depende del ambiente ni de la experiencia

invertebrate (in·VER·tuh·brit) an animal that does not have a backbone (143)
invertebrado un animal que no tiene columna vertebral

L

learned behavior (LERND bih·HAYV·yer) a behavior that has been learned from experience (153)
conducta aprendida una conducta que se ha aprendido por experiencia

lichen (LY·kuhn) a mass of fungal and algal cells that grow together in a symbiotic relationship and that are usually found on rocks or trees (103)
liquen una masa de células de hongos y de algas que crecen juntas en una relación simbiótica y que normalmente se encuentran en rocas o árboles

migration (my·GRAY·shuhn) in general, any movement of individuals or populations from one location to another; specifically, a periodic group movement that is characteristic of a given population or species (157)
migración en general, cualquier movimiento de individuos o poblaciones de un lugar a otro; específicamente, un movimiento periódico en grupo que es característico de una población o especie determinada

mutation (myoo·TAY·shuhn) a change in the nucleotide-base sequence of a gene or DNA molecule (20)
mutación un cambio en la secuencia de la base de nucleótidos de un gene o de una molécula de ADN

mycorrhiza (my·kuh·RY·zuh) a symbiotic association between fungi and plant roots (103)
micorriza una asociación simbiótica entre los hongos y las raíces de las plantas

natural selection (NACH·uhr·uhl sih·LEK·shuhn) the process by which individuals that are better adapted to their environment survive and reproduce more successfully than less-well-adapted individuals do (20)
selección natural el proceso por medio del cual los individuos que están mejor adaptados a su ambiente sobreviven y se reproducen con más éxito que los individuos menos adaptados

P-R

photosynthesis (foh·toh·SIN·thih·sis) the process by which plants, algae, and some bacteria use sunlight, carbon dioxide, and water to make food (109)
fotosíntesis el proceso por medio del cual las plantas, las algas y algunas bacterias utilizan la luz solar, el dióxido de carbono y el agua para producir alimento

pistil (PIS·tuhl) the female reproductive part of a flower that produces seeds and consists of an ovary, style, and stigma (126)
pistilo la parte reproductora femenina de una flor, la cual produce semillas y está formada por el ovario, estilo y estigma

Plantae (PLAN·tee) a kingdom made up of complex, multicellular organisms that are usually green, have cell walls made of cellulose, cannot move around, and use the sun's energy to make sugar by photosynthesis (61)
Plantae un reino formado por organismos pluricelulares complejos que normalmente son verdes, tienen una pared celular de celulosa, no tienen capacidad de movimiento y utilizan la energía del Sol para producir azúcar mediante la fotosíntesis

pollen (PAHL·uhn) the tiny granules that contain the male gametophyte of seed plants (114)
polen los gránulos diminutos que contienen el gametofito masculino en las plantas con semilla

pollination (pahl·uh·NAY·shuhn) the transfer of pollen from the male reproductive structures to the female structures of seed plants (125)
polinización la transferencia de polen de las estructuras reproductoras masculinas a las estructuras femeninas de las plantas con semillas

producer (pruh·DOO·ser) an organism that can make its own food by using energy from its surroundings (109)
productor un organismo que puede elaborar sus propios alimentos utilizando la energía de su entorno

Protista (proh·TIS·tuh) a kingdom of mostly one-celled eukaryotic organisms that are different from plants, animals, archaea, bacteria, and fungi (60, 94)
Protista un reino compuesto principalmente por organismos eucarióticos unicelulares que son diferentes de las plantas, animales, arqueas, bacterias y hongos

S

seed (SEED) a plant embryo that is enclosed in a protective coat (114)
semilla el embrión de una planta que está encerrado en una cubierta protectora

sexual reproduction (SEK·shoo·uhl ree·pruh·DUHK·shuhn) reproduction in which the sex cells from two parents unite to produce offspring that share traits from both parents (8)
reproducción sexual reproducción en la que se unen las células sexuales de los dos progenitores para producir descendencia que comparte caracteres de ambos progenitores

social behavior (SOH·shuhl bih·HAYV·yer) the interaction between animals of the same species (158)
comportamiento social la interacción entre animales de la misma especie

species (SPEE·sheez) a group of organisms that are closely related and can mate to produce fertile offspring (56)
especie un grupo de organismos que tienen un parentesco cercano y que pueden aparearse para producir descendencia fértil

spore (SPOHR) a reproductive cell or multicellular structure that is resistant to stressful environmental conditions and that can develop into an adult without fusing with another cell (97)
espora una célula reproductora o estructura pluricelular que resiste las condiciones ambientales adversas y que se puede desarrollar hasta convertirse en un adulto sin necesidad de fusionarse con otra célula

stamen (STAY·muhn) the male reproductive structure of a flower that produces pollen and consists of an anther at the tip of a filament (126)
estambre la estructura reproductora masculina de una flor, que produce polen y está formada por una antera ubicada en la punta del filamento

stimulus (STIM·yuh·luhs) anything that causes a reaction or change in an organism or any part of an organism (7, 128, 152)
estímulo cualquier cosa que causa una reacción o cambio en un organismo o cualquier parte de un organismo

T-U

territory (TEHR·ih·tohr·ee) an area that is occupied by one animal or a group of animals that do not allow other members of the species to enter (154)
territorio un área que está ocupada por un animal o por un grupo de animales que no permiten que entren otros miembros de la especie

transpiration (tran·spuh·RAY·shuhn) the process by which plants release water vapor into the air through stomata; also the release of water vapor into the air by other organisms (128)
transpiración el proceso por medio del cual las plantas liberan vapor de agua al aire por medio de los estomas; también, la liberación de vapor de agua al aire por otros organismos

tropism (TROH·piz·uhm) growth of all or part of an organism in response to an external stimulus, such as light (129)
tropismo el crecimiento de un organismo o de una parte de él en respuesta a un estímulo externo, como por ejemplo, la luz

variation (vair·ee·AY·shuhn) the occurrence of hereditary
or nonhereditary differences between different
invidivuals of a population (20)
variabilidad la incidencia de diferencias hereditarias
o no hereditarias entre distintos individuos de una
población

vascular system (VAS·kyuh·ler SIS·tuhm) a conducting
system of tissues that transport water and other
materials in plants or in animals (110)
sistema vascular un sistema de transporte de los
tejidos que lleva agua y otros materiales en las plantas
o en los animales

vertebrate (VER·tuh·brit) an animal that has a
backbone (143)
vertebrado un animal que tiene columna vertebral

virus (VY·ruhs) a nonliving, infectious particle composed
of a nucleic acid and a protein coat; it can invade and
destroy a cell (86)
virus una partícula infecciosa sin vida formada por
un ácido nucleico y una cubierta de proteína; puede
invadir una célula y destruirla

Index

Page numbers for definitions are printed in **boldface** type.
Page numbers for illustrations, maps, and charts are printed in *italics*.

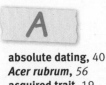